Workshop Grammar-Based Approaches to Spoken Language Processing 2007

Held in conjunction with ACL 2007

Prague, Czech Republic
29 June 2007

ISBN: 978-1-61738-527-8

Printed from e-media with permission by:

Curran Associates, Inc.
57 Morehouse Lane
Red Hook, NY 12571

Some format issues inherent in the e-media version may also appear in this print version.

Printed by Curran Associates, Inc. (2010)

For permission requests, please contact the Association for Computational Linguistics at the address below.

Association for Computational Linguistics
209 N. Eighth Street
Stroudsburg, Pennsylvania 18360

Phone: 1-570-476-8006
Fax: 1-570-476-0860

acl@aclweb.org

Additional copies of this publication are available from:

Curran Associates, Inc.
57 Morehouse Lane
Red Hook, NY 12571 USA
Phone: 845-758-0400
Fax: 845-758-2634
Email: curran@proceedings.com
Web: www.proceedings.com

Preface

Even though the statistical paradigm is dominant in research on spoken language processing, grammar based approaches are used to a great extent in industry and are also a popular choice for building command and control applications. They are particularly useful in situations where there is a lack of appropriate training data for particular domains, or even in some cases for the language as a whole, and when it is important to encode global structural constraints. Several platforms are now available that support construction of grammar-based spoken dialogue systems, including SRI's Gemini, NASA and Geneva University's Regulus and Chalmers and Gothenburg University's GF, and a variety of substantial applications have been built using these tools.

This workshop will provide an opportunity for researchers in this area to present results, compare systems and exchange practical experience in grammar based development for spoken language understanding systems.

Organizers

Chairs:

Pierrette Bouillon (Geneva University)
Manny Rayner (Powerset Inc and Geneva University)

Program Committee:

Johan Bos (La Sapienza)
Pierrette Bouillon (U Geneva)
Robin Cooper (U Gothenberg)
Jean Mark Gawron (U San Diego)
Genevieve Gorrell (U Sheffield)
Beth Ann Hockey (NASA Ames/UCSC)
Rebecca Jonson (U Gothenberg)
Hans-Ulrich Krieger (DFKI)
Oliver Lemon (U Edinburgh)
Aarne Ranta (Chalmers, Gothenberg)
Manny Rayner (Powerset/U Geneva)
Ye-Yi Wang (Microsoft)

Table of Contents

Conference Program

Wednesday, June 29, 2005

Session 1: Overview Talks

9:30–9:45 Opening Remarks

9:45–10:15 Aarne Ranta: An Overview of GF

10:15–10:45 Manny Rayner: An Overview of Regulus

10:45–11:15 Break

Session 2: GF

11:15–11:40 *Speech Recognition Grammar Compilation in Grammatical Framework*
Björn Bringert

11:40–12:05 *Converting Grammatical Framework to Regulus*
Peter Ljunglöf

12:05–12:30 *Dialogue System Localization with the GF Resource Grammar Library*
Nadine Perera and Aarne Ranta

12:30–14:30 Lunch

Session 3: Grammar-based vs statistical approaches AND applications

14:30–14:55 *Grammar-based context-specific statistical language modelling*
Rebecca Jonson

14:55–15:20 *Handling Out-of-Grammar Commands in Mobile Speech Interaction Using Backoff Filler Models*
Tim Paek, Sudeep Gandhe, Max Chickering and Yun Cheng Ju

15:20–15:45 *A Bidirectional Grammar-Based Medical Speech Translator*
Pierrette Bouillon, Glenn Flores, Marianne Starlander, Nikos Chatzichrisafis, Marianne Santaholma, Nikos Tsourakis, Manny Rayner and Beth Ann Hockey

Wednesday, June 29, 2005 (continued)

15:45–16:15 Break

Session 4: Demos and panel

16:15–17:30 Demos

A Development Environment for Building Grammar-Based Speech-Enabled Applications
Elisabeth Kron, Manny Rayner, Marianne Santaholma and Pierrette Bouillon

Björn Bringert: Generation of speech grammar formats from GF

Pierrette Bouillon and Manny Rayner: The MedSLT medical speech translator

Nadine Perera: Using GF resource grammars

17:30–18:15 Panel discussion

Speech Recognition Grammar Compilation in Grammatical Framework

Björn Bringert
Department of Computer Science and Engineering
Chalmers University of Technology and Göteborg University
SE-412 96 Göteborg, Sweden
bringert@cs.chalmers.se

Abstract

This paper describes how grammar-based language models for speech recognition systems can be generated from Grammatical Framework (GF) grammars. Context-free grammars and finite-state models can be generated in several formats: GSL, SRGS, JSGF, and HTK SLF. In addition, semantic interpretation code can be embedded in the generated context-free grammars. This enables rapid development of portable, multilingual and easily modifiable speech recognition applications.

1 Introduction

Speech recognition grammars are used for guiding speech recognizers in many applications. However, there are a number of problems associated with writing grammars in the low-level, system-specific formats required by speech recognizers. This work addresses these problems by generating speech recognition grammars and semantic interpretation components from grammars written in Grammatical Framework (GF), a high-level, type-theoretical grammar formalism. Compared to existing work on compiling unification grammars, such as Regulus (Rayner et al., 2006), our work uses a type-theoretical grammar formalism with a focus on multilinguality and modular grammar development, and supports multiple speech recognition grammar formalisms, including finite-state models.

We first outline some existing problems in the development and maintenance of speech recognition grammars, and describe how our work attempts to address these problems. In the following two sections we introduce speech recognition grammars and Grammatical Framework. The bulk of the paper then describes how we generate context-free speech recognition grammars, finite-state language models and semantic interpretation code from GF grammars. We conclude by giving references to a number of experimental dialogue systems which already use our grammar compiler for generating speech recognition grammars.

Expressivity Speech recognition grammars are written in simple formalisms which do not have the powerful constructs of high-level grammar formalisms. This makes speech recognition grammar writing labor-intensive and error prone, especially for languages with more inflection and agreement than English.

This is solved by using a high-level grammar formalism with powerful constructs and a grammar library which implements the domain-independent linguistic details.

Duplicated work When speech recognition grammars are written directly in the low-level format required by the speech recognizer, other parts of the system, such as semantic interpretation components, must often be constructed separately.

This duplicated work can be avoided by generating all the components from a single declarative source, such as a GF grammar.

Consistency Because of the lack of abstraction mechanisms and consistency checks, it is difficult

Proceedings of SPEECHGRAM 2007, pages 1–8,
Prague, Czech Republic, June 2007.

to modify a system which uses hand-written speech recognition grammars. The problem is multiplied when the system is multilingual. The developer has to modify the speech recognition grammar and the semantic interpretation component manually for each language. A simple change may require touching many parts of the grammar, and there are no automatic consistency checks.

The strong typing of the GF language enforces consistency between the semantics and the concrete representation in each language.

Localization With hand-written grammars, it is about as difficult to add support for a new language as it is to write the grammar and semantic interpretation for the first language.

GF's support for multilingual grammars and the common interface implemented by all grammars in the GF resource grammar library makes it easier to translate a grammar to a new language.

Portability A grammar in any given speech recognition grammar format cannot be used with a speech recognizer which uses another format.

In our approach, a GF grammar is used as the canonical representation which the developer works with, and speech recognition grammars in many formats can be generated automatically from this representation.

2 Speech Recognition Grammars

To achieve acceptable accuracy, speech recognition software is guided by a *language model* which defines the language which can be recognized. A language model may also assign different probabilities to different strings in the language. A language model can either be a *statistical language model (SLM)*, such as an *n*-gram model, or a *grammar-based language model*, for example a *context-free grammar (CFG)* or a *finite-state automaton (FSA)*. In this paper, we use the term *speech recognition grammar (SRG)* to refer to all grammar-based language models, including context-free grammars, regular grammars and finite-state automata.

3 Grammatical Framework

Grammatical Framework (GF) (Ranta, 2004) is a grammar formalism based on constructive type theory. In GF, an *abstract syntax* defines a semantic representation. A *concrete syntax* declares how terms in an abstract syntax are *linearized*, that is, how they are mapped to concrete representations. GF grammars can be made multilingual by having multiple concrete syntaxes for a single abstract syntax.

3.1 The Resource Grammar Library

The GF Resource Grammar Library (Ranta et al., 2006) currently implements the morphological and syntactic details of 10 languages. This library is intended to make it possible to write grammars without caring about the linguistic details of particular languages. It is inspired by *library-based software engineering*, where complex functionality is implemented in reusable software libraries with simple interfaces.

The resource grammar library is used through GF's facility for *grammar composition*, where the abstract syntax of one grammar is used in the implementation of the concrete syntax of another grammar. Thus, an application grammar writer who uses a resource grammar uses its abstract syntax terms to implement the linearizations in the application grammar.

The resource grammars for the different languages implement a common interface, i.e. they all have a common abstract syntax. This means that grammars which are implemented using resource grammars can be easily localized to other languages. Localization normally consists of translating the application-specific lexical items, and adjusting any linearizations which turn out to be unidiomatic in the language in question. For example, when the GoTGoDiS (Ericsson et al., 2006) application was localized to Finnish, only 3 out of 180 linearization rules had to be changed.

3.2 An Example GF Grammar

Figure 1 contains a small example GF abstract syntax. Figure 2 defines an English concrete syntax for it, using the resource grammar library. We will use this grammar when we show examples of speech recognition grammar generation later.

In the abstract syntax, **cat** judgements introduce syntactic categories, and **fun** judgements declare constructors in those categories. For example, the

```
abstract Food = {
  cat Order; Items; Item; Number; Size;
  fun order : Items → Order;
      and   : Items → Items → Items;
      items : Item → Number → Size → Items;
      pizza, beer  : Item;
      one, two     : Number;
      small, large : Size;
}
```

Figure 1: `Food.gf`: A GF abstract syntax module.

```
concrete FoodEng of Food = open English in {
  flags startcat = Order;
  lincat Order = Utt; Items = NP;
         Item  = CN; Number = Det;
         Size  = AP;
  lin order x     = mkUtt x;
    and x y       = mkNP and_Conj x y;
    items x n s   = mkNP n (mkCN s x);
    pizza         = mkCN (regN "pizza");
    beer          = mkCN (regN "beer");
    one           = mkDet one_Quant;
    two           = mkDet n2;
    small         = mkAP (regA "small");
    large         = mkAP (regA "large");
}
```

Figure 2: `FoodEng.gf`: English concrete syntax for the abstract syntax in Figure 1.

items constructor makes an Items term from an Item, a Number and a Size. The term *items pizza two small* is an example of a term in this abstract syntax.

In the concrete syntax, a **lincat** judgement declares the type of the concrete terms generated from the abstract syntax terms in a given category. The linearization of each constructor is declared with a **lin** judgement. In the concrete syntax in Figure 2, library functions from the English resource grammar are used for the linearizations, but it is also possible to write concrete syntax terms directly. The linearization of the term *items pizza two small* is $\{s = \text{"two small pizzas"}\}$, a record containing a single string field.

By changing the imports and the four lexical items, this grammar can be translated to any other language for which there is a resource grammar. For example, in the German version, we replace (*regN* "beer") with (*reg2N* "Bier" "Biere" *neuter*) and so on. The functions *regN* and *reg2N* implement paradigms for regular English and German nouns, respectively. This replacement can be formalized using GF's *parameterized modules*, which lets one write a common implementation that can be instantiated with the language-specific parts. Note that the application grammar does not deal with details such as agreement, as this is taken care of by the resource grammar.

4 Generating Context-free Grammars

4.1 Algorithm

GF grammars are converted to context-free speech recognition grammars in a number of steps. An overview of the compilation pipeline is show in Figure 3. The figure also includes compilation to finite-state automata, as described in Section 5. Each step of the compilation is described in more detail in the sections below.

Conversion to CFG The GF grammar is first converted into a context-free grammar annotated with functions and profiles, as described by Ljunglöf (2004).

Cycle elimination All directly and indirectly cyclic productions are removed, since they cannot be handled gracefully by the subsequent left-recursion elimination. Such productions do not contribute to the coverage to the grammar, only to the set of possible semantic results.

Bottom-up filtering Productions whose right-hand sides use categories for which there are no productions are removed, since these will never match any input.

Top-down filtering Only productions for categories which can be reached from the start category are kept. This is mainly used to remove parts of the grammar which are unused because of the choice of start category. One example where this is useful is when a speech recognition grammar is generated from a multimodal grammar (Bringert et al., 2005). In this case, the start category is different from the start category used by the parser, in that its linearization only contains the speech component of the in-

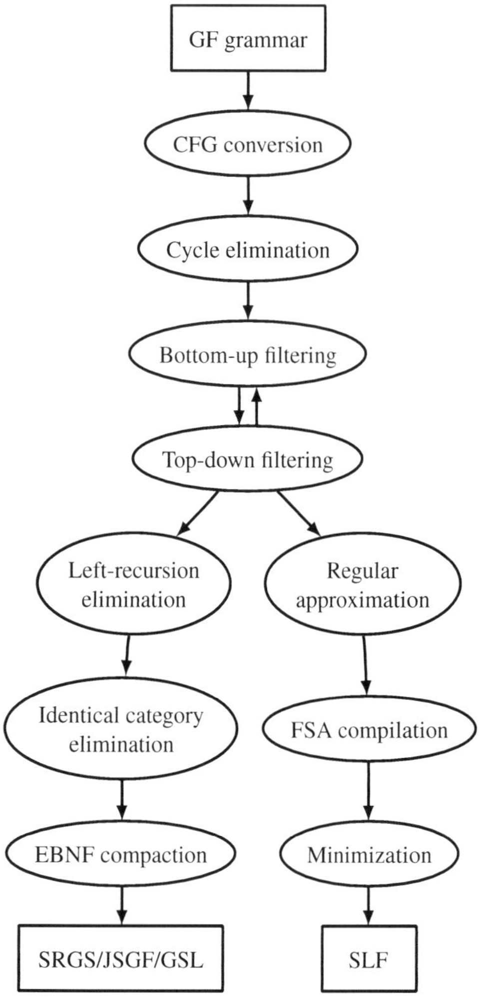

Figure 3: Grammar compilation pipeline.

put. Top-down filtering then has the effect of excluding the non-speech modalities from the speech recognition grammar.

The bottom-up and top-down filtering steps are iterated until a fixed point is reached, since both these steps may produce new filtering opportunities.

Left-recursion elimination All direct and indirect left-recursion is removed using the LC_{LR} transform described by Moore (2000). We have modified the LC_{LR} transform to avoid adding productions which use a category $A{-}X$ when there are no productions for $A{-}X$.

Identical category elimination In this step, the categories are grouped into equivalence classes by their right-hand sides and semantic annotations. The categories $A_1 \ldots A_n$ in each class are replaced by a single category $A_1{+}\ldots{+}A_n$ throughout the grammar, discarding any duplicate productions. This has the effect of replacing all categories which have identical sets of productions with a single category. Concrete syntax parameters which do not affect inflection is one source of such redundancy; the LC_{LR} transform is another.

EBNF compaction The resulting context-free grammar is compacted into an *Extended Backus-Naur Form (EBNF)* representation. This reduces the size and improves the readability of the final grammar. The compaction is done by, for each category, grouping all the productions which have the same semantic interpretation, and the same sequence of non-terminals on their right-hand sides, ignoring any terminals. The productions in each group are merged into one EBNF production, where the terminal sequences between the non-terminals are converted to regular expressions which are the unions of the original terminal sequences. These regular expressions are then minimized.

Conversion to output format The resulting non-left-recursive grammar is converted to SRGS, JSGF or Nuance GSL format.

A fragment of a SRGS ABNF grammar generated from the GF grammar in Figure 2 is shown below. The left-recursive *and* rule was removed from the grammar before compilation, as the left-recursion elimination step makes it difficult to read the generated grammar. The fragment shown here is for the singular part of the *items* rule.

```
$FE1 = $FE6 $FE9 $FE4;
$FE6 = one;
$FE9 = large | small;
$FE4 = beer  | pizza;
```

The corresponding fragment generated from the German version of the grammar is more complex, since the numeral and the adjective must agree with the gender of the noun.

```
$FG1  = $FG10 $FG13 $FG6 | $FG9 $FG12 $FG4;
$FG9  = eine;     $FG10 = ein;
$FG12 = große  | kleine;
$FG13 = großes | kleines;
$FG4  = Pizza;    $FG6 = Bier;
```

4.2 Discussion

The generated grammar is an overgenerating approximation of the original GF grammar. This is inevitable, since the GF formalism is stronger than context-free grammars, for example through its support for reduplication. GF's support for dependently typed and higher-order abstract syntax is also not yet carried over to the generated speech recognition grammars. This could be handled in a subsequent semantic interpretation step. However, that requires that the speech recognizer considers multiple hypotheses, since some may be discarded by the semantic interpretation. Currently, if the abstract syntax types are only dependent on finite types, the grammar can be expanded to remove the dependencies. This appears to be sufficient for many realistic applications.

In some cases, empty productions in the generated grammar could cause problems for the cycle and left-recursion elimination, though we have yet to encounter this in practice. Empty productions can be removed by transforming the grammar, though this has not yet been implemented.

For some grammars, the initial CFG generation can generate a very large number of productions. While the resulting speech recognition grammars are of a reasonable size, the large intermediate grammars can cause memory problems. Further optimization is needed to address this problem.

5 Finite-State Models

5.1 Algorithm

Some speech recognition systems use finite-state automata rather than context-free grammars as language models. GF grammars can be compiled to finite-state automata using the procedure shown in Figure 3. The initial part of the compilation to a finite-state model is shared with the context-free SRG compilation, and is described in Section 4.

Regular approximation The context-free grammar is approximated with a regular grammar, using the algorithm described by Mohri and Nederhof (2001).

Compilation to finite-state automata The regular grammar is transformed into a set of *non-deterministic finite automata (NFA)* using a modified version of the *make_fa* algorithm described by Nederhof (2000). For realistic grammars, applying the original *make_fa* algorithm to the whole grammar generates a very large automaton, since a copy of the sub-automaton corresponding to a given category is made for every use of the category.

Instead, one automaton is generated for each category in the regular grammar. All categories which are not in the same mutually recursive set as the category for which the automaton is generated are treated as terminal symbols. This results in a set of automata with edges labeled with either terminal symbols or the names of other automata.

If desired, the set of automata can be converted into a single automaton by substituting each category-labeled edge with a copy of the corresponding automaton. Note that this always terminates, since the sub-automata do not have edges labeled with the categories from the same mutually recursive set.

Minimization Each of the automata is turned into a minimal *deterministic finite automaton (DFA)* by using Brzozowski's (1962) algorithm, which minimizes the automaton by performing two determinizations and reversals.

Conversion to output format The resulting finite automaton can be output in HTK *Standard Lattice Format (SLF)*. SLF supports sub-lattices, which allows us to convert our set of automata directly into a set of lattices. Since SLF uses labeled nodes, rather than labeled edges, we move the labels to the nodes. This is done by first introducing a new labeled node for each edge, and then eliminating all internal unlabeled nodes. Figure 4 shows the SLF model generated from the example grammar. For clarity, the sub-lattices have been inlined.

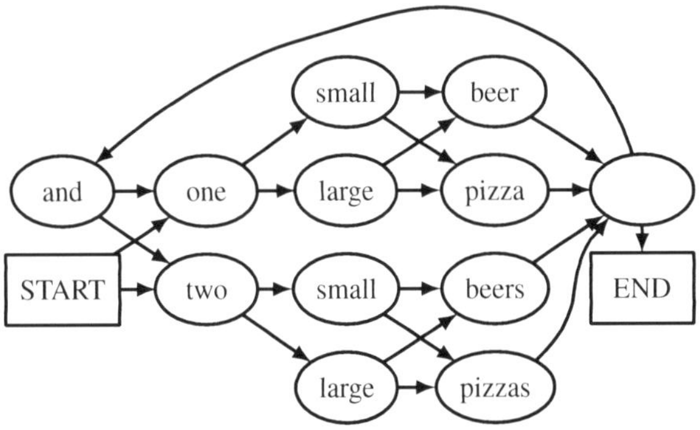

Figure 4: SLF model generated from the grammar in Figure 2.

5.2 Discussion

Finite-state models are even more restrictive than context-free grammars. This problem is handled by approximating the context-free grammar with an overgenerating finite-state automaton. This may lead to failure in a subsequent parsing step, which, as in the context-free case, is acceptable if the recognizer can return all hypotheses.

6 Semantic Interpretation

Semantic interpretation can be done as a separate parsing step after speech recognition, or it can be done with semantic information embedded in the speech recognition grammar. The latter approach resembles the *semantic actions* used by parser generators for programming languages. One formalism for semantic interpretation is the proposed *Semantic Interpretation for Speech Recognition (SISR)* standard. SISR tags are pieces of ECMAScript code embedded in the speech recognition grammar.

6.1 Algorithm

The GF system can include SISR tags when generating speech recognitions grammars in SRGS and JSGF format. The SISR tags are generated from the semantic information in the annotated CFG (Ljunglöf, 2004). The result of the semantic interpretation is an abstract syntax term.

The left-recursion elimination step makes it somewhat challenging to produce correct abstract syntax trees. We have extended Moore's (2000) LC_{LR} transform to preserve the semantic interpretation. The LC_{LR} transform introduces new categories of the form A–X where X is a proper left corner of a category A. The new category A–X can be understood as "the category A, but missing an initial X". Thus the semantic interpretation for a production in A–X is the semantic interpretation for the original A-production, abstracted (in the λ-calculus sense) over the semantic interpretation of the missing X. Conversely, where-ever a category A–X is used, its result is applied to the interpretation of the occurrence of X.

6.2 Discussion

As discussed in Section 4.2, the semantic interpretation code could be used to implement the non-context-free features of GF, but this is not yet done.

The slot-filling mechanism in the GSL format could also be used to build semantic representations, by returning program code which can then be executed. The UNIANCE grammar compiler (Bos, 2002) uses that approach.

7 Related Work

7.1 Unification Grammar Compilation

Compilation of unification grammars to speech recognition grammars is well described in the literature (Moore, 1999; Dowding et al., 2001). Regulus (Rayner et al., 2006) is perhaps the most ambitious such system. Like GF, Regulus uses a general grammar for each language, which is specialized to a domain-specific one. Ljunglöf (Ljunglöf, 2007b) relates GF and Regulus by showing how to convert GF grammars to Regulus grammars. We carry compositional semantic interpretation through left-recursion elimination using the same idea as the UNIANCE grammar compiler (Bos, 2002), though our version handles both direct and indirect left-recursion.

The main difference between our work and the existing compilers is that we work with type-theoretical grammars rather than unification grammars. While the existing work focuses on GSL as the output language, we also support a number of other formats, including finite-state models. By using the GF resource grammars, speech recognition language models can be produced for more languages than with previous systems. One shortcoming of our system is that it does not yet have support for weighted grammars.

7.2 Generating SLMs from GF Grammars

Jonson (2006) has shown that in addition to generating grammar-based language models, GF can be used to build statistical language models (SLMs). It was found that compared to our grammar-based approach, use of generated SLMs improved the recognition performance for out-of-grammar utterances significantly.

8 Results

Speech recognition grammars generated from GF grammars have already been used in a number of research dialogue systems.

GOTTIS (Bringert et al., 2005; Ericsson et al., 2006), an experimental multimodal and multilingual dialogue system for public transportation queries, uses GF grammars for parsing multimodal input. For speech recognition, it uses GSL grammars generated from the speech modality part of the GF grammars.

DJ-GoDiS, GoDiS-deLUX, and GoTGoDiS (Ericsson et al., 2006) are three applications which use GF grammars for speech recognition and parsing together with the GoDiS implementation of issue-based dialogue management (Larsson, 2002). GoTGoDiS has been translated to 7 languages using the GF resource grammar library, with each new translation taking less than one day (Ericsson et al., 2006).

The DICO (Villing and Larsson, 2006) dialogue system for trucks has recently been modified to use GF grammars for speech recognition and parsing (Ljunglöf, 2007a).

DUDE (Lemon and Liu, 2006) and its extension REALL-DUDE (Lemon et al., 2006b) are environments where non-experts can develop dialogue systems based on Business Process Models describing the applications. From keywords, prompts and answer sets defined by the developer, the system generates a GF grammar. This grammar is used for parsing input, and for generating a language model in SLF or GSL format.

The Voice Programming system by Georgila and Lemon (Georgila and Lemon, 2006; Lemon et al., 2006a) uses an SLF language model generated from a GF grammar.

Perera and Ranta (2007) have studied how GF grammars can be used for localization of dialogue systems. A GF grammar was developed and localized to 4 other languages in significantly less time than an equivalent GSL grammar. They also found the GSL grammar generated by GF to be much smaller than the hand-written GSL grammar.

9 Conclusions

We have shown how GF grammars can be compiled to several common speech recognition grammar formats. This has helped decrease development time, improve modifiability, aid localization and enable portability in a number of experimental dialogue systems.

Several systems developed in the TALK and DICO projects use the same GF grammars for speech recognition, parsing and multimodal fusion (Ericsson et al., 2006). Using the same grammar for multiple system components **reduces development and modification costs**, and makes it easier to **maintain consistency** within the system.

The feasibility of **rapid localization** of dialogue systems which use GF grammars has been demonstrated in the GoTGoDiS (Ericsson et al., 2006) system, and in experiments by Perera and Ranta (2007).

Using speech recognition grammars generated by GF makes it easy to **support different speech recognizers**. For example, by using the GF grammar compiler, the DUDE (Lemon and Liu, 2006) system can support both the ATK and Nuance recognizers.

Implementations of the methods described in this paper are freely available as part of the GF distribution[1].

Acknowledgments

Aarne Ranta, Peter Ljunglöf, Rebecca Jonson, David Hjelm, Ann-Charlotte Forslund, Håkan Burden, Xingkun Liu, Oliver Lemon, and the anonymous referees have contributed valuable comments on the grammar compiler implementation and/or this article. We would like to thank Nuance Communications, Inc., OptimSys, s.r.o., and Opera Software ASA for software licenses and technical support. The code in this paper has been typeset using `lhs2TeX`, with help from Andres Löh. This work has been partly funded by the EU TALK project, IST-507802.

References

Johan Bos. 2002. Compilation of unification grammars with compositional semantics to speech recognition packages. In *Proceedings of the 19th international conference on Computational linguistics*, pages 1–7, Morristown, NJ, USA. Association for Computational Linguistics.

Björn Bringert, Robin Cooper, Peter Ljunglöf, and Aarne Ranta. 2005. Multimodal Dialogue System Grammars. In *Proceedings of DIALOR'05, Ninth Workshop on the Semantics and Pragmatics of Dialogue*, pages 53–60.

[1] `http://www.cs.chalmers.se/~aarne/GF/`

Janusz A. Brzozowski. 1962. Canonical regular expressions and minimal state graphs for definite events. In *Mathematical theory of Automata*, Volume 12 of MRI Symposia Series, pages 529–561. Polytechnic Press, Polytechnic Institute of Brooklyn, N.Y.

John Dowding, Beth A. Hockey, Jean M. Gawron, and Christopher Culy. 2001. Practical issues in compiling typed unification grammars for speech recognition. In *ACL '01: Proceedings of the 39th Annual Meeting on Association for Computational Linguistics*, pages 164–171, Morristown, NJ, USA. Association for Computational Linguistics.

Stina Ericsson, Gabriel Amores, Björn Bringert, Håkan Burden, Ann C. Forslund, David Hjelm, Rebecca Jonson, Staffan Larsson, Peter Ljunglöf, Pilar Manchón, David Milward, Guillermo Pérez, and Mikael Sandin. 2006. Software illustrating a unified approach to multimodality and multilinguality in the in-home domain. Technical Report 1.6, TALK Project.

Kallirroi Georgila and Oliver Lemon. 2006. Programming by Voice: enhancing adaptivity and robustness of spoken dialogue systems. In *BRANDIAL'06, Proceedings of the 10th Workshop on the Semantics and Pragmatics of Dialogue*, pages 199–200.

Rebecca Jonson. 2006. Generating Statistical Language Models from Interpretation Grammars in Dialogue Systems. In *Proceedings of EACL'06.*

Staffan Larsson. 2002. *Issue-based Dialogue Management.* Ph.D. thesis, Göteborg University.

Oliver Lemon and Xingkun Liu. 2006. DUDE: a Dialogue and Understanding Development Environment, mapping Business Process Models to Information State Update dialogue systems. In *EACL 2006, 11st Conference of the European Chapter of the Association for Computational Linguistics.*

Oliver Lemon, Kallirroi Georgila, David Milward, and Tommy Herbert. 2006a. Programming Devices and Services. Technical Report 2.3, TALK Project.

Oliver Lemon, Xingkun Liu, Daniel Shapiro, and Carl Tollander. 2006b. Hierarchical Reinforcement Learning of Dialogue Policies in a development environment for dialogue systems: REALL-DUDE. In *BRANDIAL'06, Proceedings of the 10th Workshop on the Semantics and Pragmatics of Dialogue*, pages 185–186, September.

Peter Ljunglöf. 2004. *Expressivity and Complexity of the Grammatical Framework.* Ph.D. thesis, Göteborg University, Göteborg, Sweden.

Peter Ljunglöf. 2007a. Personal communication, March.

Peter Ljunglöf. 2007b. Converting Grammatical Framework to Regulus.

Mehryar Mohri and Mark J. Nederhof. 2001. Regular Approximation of Context-Free Grammars through Transformation. In Jean C. Junqua and Gertjan van Noord, editors, *Robustness in Language and Speech Technology*, pages 153–163. Kluwer Academic Publishers, Dordrecht.

Robert C. Moore. 1999. Using Natural-Language Knowledge Sources in Speech Recognition. In K. M. Ponting, editor, *Computational Models of Speech Pattern Processing*, pages 304–327. Springer.

Robert C. Moore. 2000. Removing left recursion from context-free grammars. In *Proceedings of the first conference on North American chapter of the Association for Computational Linguistics*, pages 249–255, San Francisco, CA, USA. Morgan Kaufmann Publishers Inc.

Mark J. Nederhof. 2000. Regular Approximation of CFLs: A Grammatical View. In Harry Bunt and Anton Nijholt, editors, *Advances in Probabilistic and other Parsing Technologies*, pages 221–241. Kluwer Academic Publishers.

Nadine Perera and Aarne Ranta. 2007. An Experiment in Dialogue System Localization with the GF Resource Grammar Library.

Aarne Ranta, Ali El Dada, and Janna Khegai. 2006. The GF Resource Grammar Library, June.

Aarne Ranta. 2004. Grammatical Framework: A Type-Theoretical Grammar Formalism. *Journal of Functional Programming*, 14(2):145–189, March.

Manny Rayner, Beth A. Hockey, and Pierrette Bouillon. 2006. *Putting Linguistics into Speech Recognition: The Regulus Grammar Compiler.* CSLI Publications, Ventura Hall, Stanford University, Stanford, CA 94305, USA, July.

Jessica Villing and Staffan Larsson. 2006. Dico: A Multimodal Menu-based In-vehicle Dialogue System. In *BRANDIAL'06, Proceedings of the 10th Workshop on the Semantics and Pragmatics of Dialogue*, pages 187–188.

Converting Grammatical Framework to Regulus

Peter Ljunglöf
Department of Linguistics
Göteborg University
Gothenburg, Sweden
peb@ling.gu.se

Abstract

We present an algorithm for converting Grammatical Framework grammars (Ranta, 2004) into the Regulus unification-based framework (Rayner et al., 2006). The main purpose is to take advantage of the Regulus-to-Nuance compiler for generating optimized speech recognition grammars. But there is also a theoretical interest in knowing how similar the two grammar formalisms are.

Since Grammatical Framework is more expressive than Regulus, the resulting Regulus grammars can be overgenerating. We therefore describe a subclass of Grammatical Framework for which the algorithm results in an equivalent Regulus grammar.

1 Background

In this section we describe the grammar formalism Grammatical Framework (GF), and discuss its expressive power and the present options for creating speech recognition grammars (SRGs). The main problem is that the size of the grammar can explode when inflectional parameters are expanded. In this paper we try to solve this problem by converting to a formalism for which there is an optimized SRG compiler. This formalism is Regulus, which is described together with its SRG compiler.

The formal details are left out of the descriptions in this section and can instead be found in section 2. In section 3 the conversion algorithm is presented in detail, and in section 4 there is a short discussion.

1.1 Grammatical Framework

Grammatical Framework (Ranta, 2004) is a grammar formalism based on type theory. The main feature is the separation of abstract and concrete syntax, which makes it very suitable for writing multilingual grammars. A rich module system also facilitates grammar writing as an engineering task, by reusing common grammars.

1.1.1 Separating abstract and concrete syntax

The main idea of GF is the separation of abstract and concrete syntax, a distinction which is shared with several other grammar formalisms such as Abstract Categorial Grammars (de Groote, 2001), Lambda Grammar (Muskens, 2003) and Higher Order Grammar (Pollard, 2004). The abstract part of a grammar defines a set of abstract syntactic structures, called abstract terms or trees; and the concrete part defines a relation between abstract structures and concrete structures.

GF has a *linearization* perspective to grammar writing, where the relation between abstract and concrete is viewed as a mapping from abstract to concrete structures, called linearization terms. In some cases the mapping can be partial or even many-valued.

Although not exploited in many well-known grammar formalisms, a clear separation between abstract and concrete syntax gives some advantages.

High-level language descriptions: When describing the abstract syntax, the grammar writer can choose not to care about language specific details, such as inflection and word order.

Multilingual grammars: It is possible to define different concrete syntaxes for one particular

Proceedings of SPEECHGRAM 2007, pages 9–16,
Prague, Czech Republic, June 2007.

also to simplify localization of language technology applications.

Resource grammars: The abstract syntax of one grammar can be used as a concrete syntax of another grammar. This makes it possible to implement grammar resources to be used in several different application domains.

These points are currently exploited in the GF Resource Grammar Library (Ranta et al., 2006), which is a multilingual GF grammar with a common abstract syntax for 13 languages. The grammatical coverage is similar to the Core Language Engine (Rayner et al., 2000). The main purpose of the Grammar Library is as a resource for writing domain-specific grammars.

1.1.2 Abstract syntax

The abstract theory of GF is a version of Martin-Löf's (1984) dependent type theory. A grammar consists of declarations of categories and functions. Categories can depend on other categories. Function declarations can bind variables to be used in dependent types, and also take functions as arguments, thus giving rise to higher-order functions. Since the abstract syntax also permits function definitions, the expressive power of GF abstract syntax is Turing-complete.

In this article we restrict ourselves to an important subclass of GF, where there are no dependent types and no higher-order functions. This subclass is called *context-free GF*, and is an instance of Generalized Context-Free Grammar (Pollard, 1984).

The abstract syntax of a context-free GF grammar consists of a set of function typings of the form

$$f \quad : \quad A_1 \to \cdots \to A_\delta \to A$$

This typing says that f is a function taking δ arguments with categories $A_1 \ldots A_\delta$ and returning a category A. This is equivalent to a context-free grammar without terminal symbols. Note however, that the function f would be written $A \to A_1 \ldots A_\delta$ as an ordinary context-free rule. I.e., the left-hand side of a context-free rule corresponds to the result of the function, which is written to the right. The restriction to a context-free backbone is not severe, since the concrete syntax is so expressive.

1.1.3 Concrete syntax

Linearizations are written as terms in a typed functional programming language, which is limited to ensure decidability in generation and in parsing. The language has records and finite-domain functions (called tables); and the basic types are terminal lists (called strings) and finite data types (called parameter types). There are also local definitions, lambda-abstractions and global function definitions. The parameters are declared by the grammar; they can be hierarchical but not recursive, to ensure finiteness.

The language of linearization terms is quite complex, but it can be compiled to a normalized form which is called canonical GF. In this paper we assume that all linearizations are in canonical form. A canonical concrete GF grammar contains declarations of all parameter types, and linearization definitions for all abstract functions.

1.1.4 Expressive power

The expressive power of context-free GF solely depends on the possibility of discontinuous constituents. This means that one grammatical phrase can be split into several parts occurring in different places in the sentence. Discontinuous constituents permit a simple and compositional way of treating, e.g., German compound verbs, where the particle commonly is moved to the end of the sentence.

Ljunglöf (2004) showed that context-free GF is equivalent to Multiple Context-Free Grammar (Seki et al., 1991), which is known to be parseable in time polynomial in the length of the input string. From a converted Multiple CFG, each constituent can be extracted as a context-free rule, which will result in a possibly overgenerating context-free grammar. This context-free grammar can be output from the GF system in several different speech recognition formats, as described by Bringert (2007).

There is a severe problem with the conversion from GF to Multiple CFG however – the size of the resulting grammar tend to explode when the inflectional parameters are expanded. Large grammars such as many of the languages in the Resource

Grammar Library simply cannot be converted. One solution would be to optimize the conversion algorithm, e.g., by interleaving parameter expansion and grammar compaction. Another solution would be to translate into a grammar formalism which does not have this size explosion. This is where Regulus comes in – if we could translate GF grammars into Regulus grammars, we could make use of the research already put into the Regulus-to-Nuance compiler, and would not have to reinvent the wheel.

1.2 Regulus

Regulus is an open-source toolkit for writing grammar-based speech recognition systems (Rayner et al., 2006).[1] The central part is the Regulus grammar formalism and a compiler for creating speech recognition grammars. The toolkit has been enhanced with templates for developing e.g., speech translation systems and dialogue systems. There is also an English resource grammar, which can be used for grammar specialization using explanation-based learning (Rayner et al., 2006, chapters 9–10).

1.2.1 Unification of finite parameters

The Regulus formalism is a context-free grammar, enhanced with unification of finite parameters. This means that the formalism is equivalent to a context-free grammar.

Each context-free category (e.g., Noun) has a number of features (e.g., Number and Gender) with a finite domain of values (e.g., Sg/Pl and Masc/Fem/Neutr). The feature values are specified using a record paired with the grammatical category. Logical variables can be used for unifying features of different constituents in the rule. It is possible to define macros for simplifying common tasks, e.g., when implementing a lexicon.

Compared to Grammatical Framework, the Regulus formalism is quite restricted. There is no clear distinction between abstract and concrete syntax, and there is no advanced module system in which to define grammatical resources. Also, Regulus lacks discontinuous constituents, which reduces the expressive power considerably.

[1]More information about Regulus, including download information, can be found on the project homepage: `http://www.issco.unige.ch/projects/regulus/`

1.2.2 Compiling Regulus to Nuance GSL

Nuance Communications (2003) has developed a context-free grammar format for speech recognition, which has become one of the de facto standards for speech recognition. The grammar format is called Nuance Grammar Specification Language (GSL). The format has some special features, such as semantic tagging and probabilistic grammar rules. There are also restrictions in the format, most notably that the grammars must not be left-recursive.

The Regulus formalism is designed to be able to make use of the special features in Nuance GSL, and the compiler can always create correct GSL grammars without left-recursion.

2 Formal definitions

In this section we give formal definitions of rules and linearization terms in GF, grammar rules and terms in Regulus, and the intermediate structures we will be using.

2.1 GF grammar rules

Since we are only interested in GF grammars with a context-free backbone, the abstract syntax is a context-free grammar where each rule has a unique name. The rules are written as typings in a functional language:

$$f \quad : \quad A_1 \rightarrow \cdots \rightarrow A_\delta \rightarrow A$$

As mentioned earlier, this declaration corresponds to the context-free rule $A \rightarrow A_1 \ldots A_\delta$.

Linearizations are written as function definitions, $f\, x_1 \ldots x_\delta = t$, where $x_1 \ldots x_\delta$ are variables that occur in the linearization term t. An alternative way of writing this is to name the variables consistently for each rule, and then the linearization term t itself is sufficient as a linearization definition. We adopt this idea and use the uniform variable names $\$1 \ldots \$\delta$ in each linearization. With this approach we also distinguish the argument variables from the parameter variables which get bound in tables.

2.2 GF linearization terms and substructures

A parameter type P is just a set of parameter values $\{\mathsf{p}_1, \ldots, \mathsf{p}_n\}$. Note that all parameter types must be disjoint, i.e., each parameter should belong to exactly one parameter type. Linearizations are defined by association linearization terms to the abstract functions. Note that the definition of terms is slightly more general than the definition in GF, since we want to include reduced terms in the definition. The relation between the introduced classes are as follows:

$$\left.\begin{array}{r}\mathbb{P} \subset \mathbb{V}_{\mathbf{Par}} \\ \mathbb{V}_{\mathbf{Str}}\end{array}\right\} \subset \mathbb{V} \subset \mathbb{T}$$

Terms ($t \in \mathbb{T}$) are defined inductively as follows:

$$\begin{array}{rcll} t & ::= & \$n & \text{argument} \\ & | & "s" & \text{string} \\ & | & t +\!\!+ t' & \text{concatenation} \\ & | & p & \text{pattern} \\ & | & \{r_1 = t_1; \ldots; r_n = t_n\} & \text{record} \\ & | & t.r & \text{projection} \\ & | & [p_1 \Rightarrow t_1; \ldots; p_n \Rightarrow t_n] & \text{table} \\ & | & t_1!t_2 & \text{selection} \end{array}$$

where $n > 0$ is a positive integer, $p \in \mathbb{P}$ is a pattern, and $r \in \mathbb{R}$ is a record label. The class $\mathbb{R}$ of record labels is just a finite class of atomic values. The argument reference $\$n$ denotes the nth argument of the linearization function.

Patterns ($p \in \mathbb{P}$) are pairs $x@\pi$ of variables, x, and sets of parameters, $\pi = \{\mathsf{p}_1 \ldots \mathsf{p}_n\}$. The parameters $\mathsf{p}_1 \ldots \mathsf{p}_n$ all must belong to the same parameter type P, i.e., $\pi \subseteq \mathsf{P}$. The meaning of the pattern is that x is bound to one of the parameters in π. If $\pi = \mathsf{P}$ we can skip that part and simply write x. Conversely, if x is not used elsewhere in the term, we can skip it and simply write π.

Note that a pattern is a term in itself, but in GF it will always occur as a single variable x or as a single parameter p. However, after the conversion algorithm has transformed tables into records, patterns will become first class terms.

Reduced terms ($v \in \mathbb{V}$) are subterms of ordinary terms. A reduced term is a term which does not contain a table or a selection, and where projections only occur in the form $\$n.\rho$, where $\rho \in \mathbb{R}^*$ is a sequence of labels:

$$\begin{array}{rcl} v & ::= & \$n.\rho \\ & | & "s" \\ & | & v +\!\!+ v' \\ & | & p \\ & | & \{r_1 = v_1; \ldots; r_n = v_n\} \end{array}$$

Reduced parameter terms ($v_p \in \mathbb{V}_{\mathbf{Par}}$) are subterms of reduced terms, which correspond to parameters:

$$v_p \quad ::= \quad \$n.\rho \quad | \quad p$$

Reduced string terms ($v_s \in \mathbb{V}_{\mathbf{Str}}$) are subterms of reduced terms, which correspond to strings:

$$v_s \quad ::= \quad \$n.\rho \quad | \quad "s" \quad | \quad v_s +\!\!+ v_s'$$

Note that this is equivalent to a sequence of argument projections and string constants, which in turn is equivalent to a right-hand side in a context-free rule.

2.3 Regulus grammar rules and terms

A Regulus grammar is a unification-based phrase-structure grammar. It consists of grammar rules, which in turn is built up using Regulus terms.

Regulus rules are regular context-free grammar rules, where each category is augmented with a Regulus term:

$$A{:}v \quad \rightarrow \quad \sigma_0 \quad A_1{:}v_1 \quad \sigma_1 \quad \ldots \quad A_\delta{:}v_\delta \quad \sigma_\delta$$

where each A_i is a context-free category, each v_i is a Regulus term, and each σ_i is a (possibly empty) sequence of terminal tokens.

Regulus terms are flat records where all values are patterns ($p_i = x_i@\pi_i$):[2]

$$v_r \quad ::= \quad \{r_1 = p_1; \ldots; r_n = p_n\}$$

In this sense, Regulus terms are just subterms of reduced terms. However, a Regulus term can include one of the two special labels sem and gsem, corresponding to return values and global slot-filling in Nuance GSL, respectively. They can contain complex structures, such as deeply nested lists and records. Using these it is possible to define the syntactical structure of a phrase.

[2]This is a slight abuse of syntax – in Regulus the record row $r_i = x_i@\pi_i$ is written as two separate rows $r_i = x_i; r_i = \pi_i$.

3 Converting GF to Regulus

In this section we describe an algorithm for converting any context-free GF rule into a set of Regulus rules. This conversion is done in three steps:

1. Tables and table selections are removed from the GF term, resulting in several reduced terms and sets of constraints.
2. The results are massaged into Regulus terms for the left-hand side and the right-hand side.
3. Finally, GF abstract syntax is used to create the final Regulus rules.

In the final step, the abstract syntax is added as a semantic value in the Regulus rules. This makes it possible to get back the GF abstract syntax tree, when using Regulus (or Nuance) for parsing the grammar.

Example *As a running example we will use a standard English GF rule for combining transitive verbs with noun phrases:*

$$\begin{array}{lcl} \mathsf{vp} & : & \mathsf{TV} \to \mathsf{NP} \to \mathsf{VP} \\ & = & \{\mathsf{s} = [n \Rightarrow \$1.\mathsf{s}!n +\!\!+ \$2.\mathsf{s}]\} \end{array}$$

The idea is that a verb phrase has a parametrical number (n), which it inherits from the verb. When the verb phrase is used in a sentence, the number will depend on the inherent number of the subject.

3.1 Converting tables to unification-based records

The main difference between GF and Regulus is that the former has tables and the latter has unification. The problem when converting from GF to Regulus is therefore how to get rid of the tables and selections. We present an algorithm for removing tables and selections, by replacing them with logical variables and equality constraints.

The basic idea is to translate each row $p_i \Rightarrow t_i$ in a table into a record $\{\mathbf{p} = p_i; \mathbf{v} = t_i\}$. The variables in t_i which are bound by p_i become logical variables. Thus the original table gives rise to n different records (if n is the number of table rows), which in the end becomes n different Regulus terms.

A table selection $t!t'$ then has to be translated into the value $t.\mathbf{v}$ of the table, and a constraint is added that the selection term t' and the pattern $t.\mathbf{p}$ of the table should be unified.

Step 1: Removing tables and selections

We define a nondeterministic reduction operation $\Longrightarrow$. The meaning of $t \Longrightarrow v/\Gamma$ is that the term $t \in \mathbb{T}$ is converted to the reduced term $v \in \mathbb{V}$ together with the set of constraints $\Gamma \subseteq \mathbb{V}_{\mathbf{Par}} \times \mathbb{V}_{\mathbf{Par}}$. Each constraint in Γ is of the form $v_p \doteq v'_p$, where v_p and v'_p are reduced parameter terms.

- Each row $p_i \Rightarrow t_i$ in a table is reduced to a record containing the pattern p_i and the reduced value v_i:

$$\frac{t_i \Longrightarrow v_i/\Gamma_i}{[\ldots; p_i \Rightarrow t_i; \ldots] \Longrightarrow \{\mathbf{p} = p_i; \mathbf{v} = v_i\}/\Gamma_i}$$

  Note that this rule is nondeterministic – the table is reduced to n different terms, where n is the number of table rows.

- A table selection $t!t'$ is reduced to the value $v.\mathsf{v}$, with the added constraint that the pattern $v.\mathsf{p}$ and the selection term v' should unify:

$$\frac{t \Longrightarrow v_0/\Gamma \qquad t' \Longrightarrow v'_p/\Gamma'}{t!t' \Longrightarrow v \;/\; \Gamma\Gamma'(v_p \doteq v'_p)} \qquad \begin{array}{l} v_p = \mathbf{prj}(v_0, \mathbf{p}) \\ v \;\; = \mathbf{prj}(v_0, \mathbf{v}) \end{array}$$

  Note that since t' denotes a parameter, it will be reduced to a parameter term, $v'_p \in \mathbb{V}_{\mathbf{Par}}$.

- A record projection $t.r$ is reduced to a projection $v.r$:

$$\frac{t \Longrightarrow v/\Gamma}{t.r \Longrightarrow v_r/\Gamma} \qquad v_r = \mathbf{prj}(v, r)$$

- All other term constructors are reduced compositionally, i.e., by reducing the internal terms recursively.

The function $\mathbf{prj}(v, r)$ calculates the projection of r on the simple term v. Since there are only two reduced term constructors that can correspond to a record, there are only two cases in the definition:

$$\begin{array}{lcl} \mathbf{prj}(\{\ldots; r = v_r; \ldots\}, r) & = & v_r \\ \mathbf{prj}(\$n.\rho \qquad\qquad\quad, r) & = & \$n.\rho r \end{array}$$

Example *The original linearization term of the example contains one table and one selection. The selection* $\$1.\mathsf{s}!n$ *is reduced to* $\$1.\mathbf{sv}$ *with the added constraint* $\$1.\mathbf{sp} \doteq n$*. And since there is only one row in the table, the example term is reduced to one single term* v_{vp} *with the constraints* Γ_{vp}*:*

$$\begin{aligned} v_{\mathsf{vp}} &= \{\mathsf{s} = \{\mathbf{p} = n; \mathbf{v} = \$1.\mathbf{sv} +\!\!+ \$2.\mathsf{s}\}\} \\ \Gamma_{\mathsf{vp}} &= \$1.\mathbf{sp} \doteq n \end{aligned}$$

3.2 Building Regulus terms

The reduced term and the constraints from the first step do not constitute a Regulus grammar rule, but they have to be massaged into the correct form. This is done in four small steps below.

Step 2a: Flattening the reduced term

After the conversion $t \Longrightarrow v/\Gamma$, we have a reduced term $v \in \mathbb{V}$ and a set of constraints $\Gamma \in \mathbb{V}_{\mathbf{Par}} \times \mathbb{V}_{\mathbf{Par}}$. Now we convert v into a set of constraints and add to the constraint store Γ:

- For each subterm v' in v denoting a parameter, add $\$0.\rho \doteq v'$ to Γ. The path ρ is the sequence of labels for getting from v to v', i.e., $v' = v.\rho$.

We also create a set of "proto rules" $\Sigma \in \mathbb{R}^* \times \mathbb{V}_{\mathbf{Str}}$:

- For each subterm v' in v denoting a string, add $\rho \to v'$ to Σ. The path ρ is the same as above.

Example *There is one subterm in* v_{vp} *denoting a parameter, so we add* $\$0.\mathbf{sp} \doteq n$ *to* Γ_{vp}*. There is one subterm in* v_{vp} *that denotes a string, so we let* Σ_{vp} *contain* $\mathsf{sv} \to \$1.\mathbf{sv} +\!\!+ \$2.\mathsf{s}$.

Step 2b: Simplifying the constraints

Now we have two constraint stores, Σ and Γ, of which the latter can be partially evaluated into a simpler form.

1. For each constraint of the form $\$n_1.\rho_1 \doteq \$n_2.\rho_2$, we replace it with two new constraints $\$n_i.\rho_i \doteq x$, where x is a fresh variable.[3]
2. For each constraint of the form $x_1@\pi_1 \doteq x_2@\pi_2$, there are two possibilities:
   - If π_1 and π_2 are disjoint, then the constraint is contradictive and we remove v, Γ and Σ from the list of results.
   - Otherwise, we replace each occurrence of $x_i@\pi_i$ in v and in Γ, by $x@\pi$, where x is a fresh variable and $\pi = \pi_1 \cap \pi_2$.

[3] Recall that x is just a shorthand for $x@\pi$, where π is the set of all parameters.

Example *We do not have to do anything to* Γ_{vp}*, since all constraints already are in simplified form.*

Step 2c: Building Regulus terms

Now Γ only contains constraints of the form $\$n.\rho \doteq p$ where $p = x@\pi$. We transform these constraints into the Regulus records $T_0, T_1, \ldots, T_\delta$ in the following way:

- For each constraint $\$n.\rho \doteq p$, add the record row $\{\rho = p\}$ to T_n.

Note that the labels in the Regulus terms are sequences of GF labels.

Example *The constraints in* Γ_{vp} *now give rise to the Regulus terms:*

$$\begin{aligned} T_{\mathsf{vp},0} &= \{\mathbf{sp} = n\} \\ T_{\mathsf{vp},1} &= \{\mathbf{sp} = n\} \\ T_{\mathsf{vp},2} &= \{\} \end{aligned}$$

3.3 Building a Regulus grammar

To be able to create Regulus grammar rules from the Regulus terms $T_0 \ldots T_\delta$, we need to look at the abstract syntax in the GF grammar. In this section we will assume that the typing of the linearization in question is $f : A_1 \to \cdots \to A_\delta \to A$.

Regulus (and Nuance GSL) permits the use of arbitrary nested lists in the special sem feature. We will use the nested list for representing a GF abstract syntax tree which then will be returned directly by Nuance after the parsing has succeeded. This is important since the arguments to the function can be permuted in the linearization, which then means that the arguments in the Regulus rule are permuted as well.

Step 3a: Adding GF abstract syntax to the Regulus terms

The abstract syntax tree of the original rule is put as a sem value in the left-hand side term T_0:

- Add the row $\{\mathsf{sem}{=}[f\ x_1 \ldots x_\delta]\}$ to T_0.
- For each $1 \leq i \leq \delta$, add $\{\mathsf{sem}{=}x_i\}$ to T_i.

Note that the $x_1 \ldots x_\delta$ should be fresh variables, not used elsewhere in the terms.

Example *After adding semantics, the example terms become:*

$$
\begin{array}{rcl}
T_{\mathsf{vp},0} & = & \{\mathsf{sp} = n; \mathsf{sem} = [\mathsf{vp}\ x\ y]\} \\
T_{\mathsf{vp},1} & = & \{\mathsf{sp} = n; \mathsf{sem} = x\} \\
T_{\mathsf{vp},2} & = & \{\mathsf{sem} = y\}
\end{array}
$$

Step 3b: Building Regulus grammar rules

Finally, we can transform the proto rules in Σ into Regulus grammar rules:

- For each proto rule $\rho_0 \rightarrow v_1 +\!\!+ \cdots +\!\!+ v_m$ in Σ, create a new Regulus rule:

  $$A\,\rho_0 : T_0 \quad \rightarrow \quad v_1^\circ \ \ldots \ v_m^\circ$$

  where the terms in the right-hand side are calculated as follows:

  $$
  \begin{array}{rcl}
  (\text{"}s\text{"})^\circ & = & \text{"}s\text{"} \\
  (\$n.\rho)^\circ & = & A_n\,\rho : T_n
  \end{array}
  $$

Example *From the single proto rule in Σ_{vp} we create the Regulus rule:*

$$\mathsf{VP_{sv}} : T_{\mathsf{vp},0} \quad \rightarrow \quad \mathsf{TV_{sv}} : T_{\mathsf{vp},1} \quad \mathsf{NP_{s}} : T_{\mathsf{vp},2}$$

where the terms $T_{\mathsf{vp},i}$ are described above.

4 Discussion

We have presented an algorithm for converting GF grammars with a context-free backbone into unification-based Regulus grammars. The algorithm is simple and straightforward, which is an indication that the formalisms are more similar than one might have guessed beforehand.

4.1 Equivalence of the grammars

The presented algorithm does not necessarily yield an equivalent grammar. This is a consequence of the fact that context-free GF is equivalent to Multiple CFG, and that Multiple CFG is much more expressive than context-free grammars.

However, if the original grammar does not make use of multiple constituents, the conversion is equivalent. Note that the grammar might very well contain multiple constituents, but if there is no right-hand side that refers to both constituents simultaneously the equivalence is still preserved.

4.2 Complexity issues

As mentioned earlier, each GF function might give rise to several Regulus rules, so in one sense the resulting grammar is bigger than the original. However, the actual size in terms of memory usage does not differ (except maybe linear because of differences in syntax).

4.2.1 The number of rules

The number of Regulus rules for one single GF linearization term is equal to:

$$|\Sigma| \prod_{\phi} |\phi|$$

where $|\Sigma|$ is the number of discontinuous constituents, and ϕ ranges over all tables in the linearization term. This is easy to see, since it is only tables that are reduced nondeterministically, and each proto rule in Σ gives rise to one Regulus rule.

4.2.2 The size of the grammar

The total size of the final grammar can be larger than the original GF grammar. This is because the Regulus grammar will contain lots of copies of the same structures, e.g., everything outside of a table has to be duplicated in for each table row. The theoretical limit is the same as above – the number of constituents, times the the total product of all table rows – but in practice the grammar explosion is not that extreme.

Since the increase in size is due to copying, the Regulus grammar can be compacted by the use of macros (Rayner et al., 2006, section 4.5). This could probably be implemented in the algorithm directly, but we have not yet investigated this idea.

4.2.3 Time complexity

The time complexity of the algorithm is approximately equivalent to the size of the resulting Regulus grammar. The first step (in section 3.1), can be implemented as a single pass through the term and is therefore linear in the size of the resulting terms. The post-processing steps (in section 3.2) are also linear in the size of the terms and constraints. Finally, the steps for building grammar rules does not depend on the term size at all. Thus, the time complexity is linear in the size of the final Regulus grammar.

4.3 Using Regulus as a compiler for speech recognition grammars

By presenting an algorithm for converting GF grammars into Regulus, it is possible to further use the Regulus-to-Nuance compiler for getting an optimized speech recognition grammar. The advantage to compiling Nuance grammars directly from GF is clear: the Regulus project has developed and implemented several optimizations (Rayner et al., 2006, chapter 8), which would have to be reimplemented in a direct GF-to-Nuance compiler.

As previously mentioned in section 1.1.4, there is a speech recognition grammar compiler already implemented in GF (Bringert, 2007), which uses the equivalence of GF and Multiple CFG. An interesting future investigation would be to compare the two approaches on realistic grammars.

References

Björn Bringert. 2007. Speech recognition grammar compilation in Grammatical Framework. Submitted to SpeechGram 2007.

Philippe de Groote. 2001. Towards abstract categorial grammars. In *39th Meeting of the Association for Computational Linguistics*, Toulouse, France.

Peter Ljunglöf. 2004. *Expressivity and Complexity of the Grammatical Framework*. Ph.D. thesis, Göteborg University and Chalmers University of Technology, November.

Per Martin-Löf. 1984. *Intuitionistic Type Theory*. Bibliopolis, Napoli.

Reinhard Muskens. 2003. Language, lambdas, and logic. In Geert-Jan Kruijff and Richard Oehrle, editors, *Resource Sensitivity in Binding and Anaphora*, pages 23–54. Kluwer.

Nuance Communications, Inc., 2003. *Nuance Speech Recognition System 8.5: Grammar Developer's Guide*, December.

Carl Pollard. 1984. *Generalised Phrase Structure Grammars, Head Grammars and Natural Language*. Ph.D. thesis, Stanford University.

Carl Pollard. 2004. Higher-order categorial grammar. In Michel Moortgat, editor, *International Conference on Categorial Grammars*, Montpellier, France.

Aarne Ranta, Ali El-Dada, and Janna Khegai, 2006. *The GF Resource Grammar Library*. Can be downloaded from the GF homepage `http://www.cs.chalmers.se/~aarne/GF`

Aarne Ranta. 2004. Grammatical Framework, a type-theoretical grammar formalism. *Journal of Functional Programming*, 14(2):145–189.

Manny Rayner, Dave Carter, Pierrette Bouillon, Vassilis Digalakis, and Mats Wirén. 2000. *The Spoken Language Translator*. Cambridge University Press.

Manny Rayner, Beth Ann Hockey, and Pierrette Bouillon. 2006. *Putting Linguistics into Speech Recognition: The Regulus Grammar Compiler*. CSLI Publications.

Hiroyuki Seki, Takashi Matsumara, Mamoru Fujii, and Tadao Kasami. 1991. On multiple context-free grammars. *Theoretical Computer Science*, 88:191–229.

Dialogue System Localization with the GF Resource Grammar Library

Nadine Perera
Department of Man Machine Interaction
BMW Group Research and Technology
Munich, Germany
nadine.perera@bmw.de

Aarne Ranta
Department of Computing Science
Chalmers University of Technology
and Göteborg University
Gothenburg, Sweden
aarne@cs.chalmers.se

Abstract

We present two experiments in the localization of spoken dialogue systems. The domain of the dialogue system is an MP3 application for automobiles. In the first experiment, a grammar in Nuance GSL format was rewritten in Grammatical Framework (GF). Within GF, the grammar was extended from two to six languages, giving a baseline for semantically complete grammars. In the second experiment, the German version of this baseline GF grammar was extended with the goal to restore the coverage of the original Nuance grammar.

1 Credits

Part of this work was done under the TALK[1] research project, funded by EU FP6 [ref. 507802]. The Nuance grammar was written by Jochen Steigner, Peter Poller, and Rosemary Stegmann. The first GF experiment was made together with Björn Bringert. The Spanish grammar was written together with Libertad Tansini.

2 Introduction

Spoken dialogue systems for cars emerged in the late 1990s with the appearance of advanced information and communication systems. Driving a car is a classical visual manual task, as the driver should keep his hands on the steering wheel and his glance on the surrounding traffic and the street. Speech interaction is very well-suited for secondary-level tasks such as handling information and entertainment systems.

The current spoken dialogue system in the automobiles of the BMW Group is a Command&Control-based system (Hagen et al., 2004). For the interaction with the entertainment and information functions of the iDrive system (Haller, 2003), the paradigm pursued is You-Can-Speak-What-You-See, i.e. every menu item or option that is shown on screen can be spoken. The localization of that spoken dialogue system for currently eight languages is done manually by translators, without advanced automation methods or special tools. The Command&Control-based approach has its disadvantages, as the system can only handle a fix set of commands. This makes it difficult for system novices to interact with the dialogue system because they may not know the commands they need to say to reach their goal.

Advanced conversational dialogue systems that allow a more flexible input and let the user decide about the form and the amount of the communicated information are being investigated. In order to implement such a flexible spoken dialogue system in the automobiles of the BMW Group, not only one dialogue system, but at least eight would have to be built - one for each language. The different, localized versions of the system would have to be designed in a way that allows for the generic addition of use cases, i.e. changes and additions to the German grammar (which is viewed as the initial source grammar) must be ported to the localized versions consistently and without the need to change the whole localized grammar.

2.1 Grammar Writing

Linguistic experts who write grammars for companies whose focus is not in language technology usually have to possess profound technical competence and programming skills in addition to linguistic expertise. For those grammar engineers who are computer scientists or engineers with little university ed-

[1] Tools for Ambient Linguistic Knowledge, www.talk-project.org

Proceedings of SPEECHGRAM 2007, pages 17–24,
Prague, Czech Republic, June 2007.

ucation in linguistics, a programming paradigm enabling them to avoid dealing with the morphological inflection paradigms of several languages would certainly be welcome. Writing consistent grammars for multiple languages is quite challenging: Writing one grammar requires the grammar engineer to be at least a fluent speaker of the language the grammar covers. If he also knows another language quite well, he may be able to localize a grammar from that language to his native language. This implies that for every language which requires a localized grammar, a person who knows the source language and is a native speaker of the target language is needed. At the moment, there is no commercial tool available that helps grammar engineers with the localization of spoken dialogue systems.

2.2 The Nuance SAMMIE grammar

Within the TALK project, an in-car spoken dialogue system for the MP3 domain was created and integrated into a BMW 3-Series Coupe (Becker et al., 2007). For the speech understanding component, a German corpus named SAMMIE (SAarbrücken Multi-Modal Interface Experiment) was collected by Saarland University and DFKI[2] using a Wizard of Oz experiment.

A grammar in Nuance GSL format was written to specify well-formed sentences complying with the corpus data. The GSL formalism is a variant of BNF (context-free grammar), with Extended BNF additions such as disjunctions and Kleene closures. The grammar was structured according to syntactical motivations and interaction type coherence. To minimize overgeneration, nonterminals were instantiated with usual grammatical features. For instance, genitive definite forms of artist expressions were generated by the disjunction

```
NP_ARTIST_CASE_GEN[
 (DET_NUM_SING_CASE_GEN_GEND_NEUT
  N_ARTIST_NUM_SING_CASE_GEN_GEND_MASC)
 (DET_NUM_SING_CASE_GEN_GEND_FEM
  N_ARTIST_NUM_SING_CASE_DATIV_GEND_FEM)]
```

For a more detailed description of the grammar, see (Becker et al., 2007).

The German Sammie grammar in Nuance format (NuanceGer) was checked and extended continuously while the dialogue system was built. User evaluation results were analyzed and missing utterances were added to the grammar. In addition to that, an English version of the grammar, called "NuanceEng" here, was built by a near-native speaker of English. This grammar is the starting point for our experiments. Figure 1 shows a graph of the grammar development for the first experiment, Figure 2 for the second experiment.

[2] German Research Center for Artificial Intelligence

2.3 Outline of the paper

Section 3 gives an introduction to GF and its resource grammar library, by working through the implementation of a fragment of the Sammie grammar. Section 4 describes the first experiment, in which a baseline Sammie grammar was ported to six languages. Section 5 describes the second experiment, in which the German grammar was extended towards the coverage of the original grammar. Section 6 concludes with statistics on the experiments, related work, and some general lessons learnt.

3 Multilingual grammars in GF

GF (Grammatical Framework, (Ranta, 2004)) is a grammar formalism based on ideas from type theory and functional programming. Originally designed for written technical documents, GF focuses on language-independent semantic representations and their multilingual renderings. These features have proved useful in dialogue systems as well, and a support for dialogue applications is completed by translators from GF to various speech recognition formats, such as Nuance (Bringert, 2007).

A **grammar**, in the sense of GF, has an **abstract syntax** and a set of **concrete syntaxes**. The abstract syntax is a semantic description of an application domain. Each concrete syntax is a mapping of the semantics into a language, typically a natural language. To give an example from the GF implementation of the Sammie grammar, the abstract syntax has objects such as

```
identify ( currently_playing_object )
```

The six concrete syntaxes map the abstract object into the strings

```
vad heter den här sången
wie heißt dieses lied
comment s'appelle cette chanson
como se llama esta canción
mikä on tämän laulun nimi
what is the name of this song
```

of Swedish, German, French, Spanish, Finnish, and English, respectively.

The abstract syntax is specified by a set of **categories** (`cat`) and **constructor functions** (`fun`), in the same way as an inductive family of datatypes in a functional programming language. Here is a fragment of the Sammie abstract syntax, with five categories and five constructor functions:

```
cat
  Action ; ToIdentify ; Object ;
  Playlist ; Artist ;
fun
  create : Action ;
  identify : ToIdentify -> Action ;
  play : Object -> Action ;
  remove : Playlist -> Object -> Action ;
  currently_playing_object : ToIdentify ;
```

The concrete syntax is specified by defining a **linearization type** (`lincat`) for each category, as well as a **linearization function** (`lin`) for each constructor. A baseline concrete syntax can be obtained by just assigning the type of strings to each category, and defining:

```
lincat
  Action, ToIdentify,
  Object, Playlist, Artist = Str ;
lin
  create = ["create a new playlist"] ;
  identify x = x ;
  play = "play" ++ x :
  remove x y = "remove"++ y ++"from"++ x ;
  currently_playing_object =
    ["what is the name of this song"] ;
```

A concrete syntax like this is essentially a system of templates with chunks of canned text. While it is easy to produce for small applications, it does not scale up well, especially in languages that have rich morphology and require agreement in syntactic structures. Thus GF also supports user-defined **parameter types**, which can be used to control inflection and word order in linearization. For instance, the German version of the above grammar needs a type of Case, and the linearization of `Object` and `Playlist` depends on case:

```
lincat
  Object, Playlist = Case => Str ;
lin
  remove x y = "nimm" ++ y ! Acc ++
    "aus" ++ x ! Dat ++ "heraus"
```

3.1 The GF resource grammar library

Having to think about parameters requires linguistic knowledge from the grammar writer. Moreover, accurate descriptions tend to become long and complex. The GF solution to this problem is a **resource grammar library**. Like any software library, this library can be used via a high-level API (an abstract syntax for linguistic structures) that hides the implementation details (the concrete syntaxes for each language). The GF resource grammar library is currently available for 10–15 languages (10 languages support the full API, 5 just parts of it). Its first applications were in the domain of written technical language (Burke and Johannisson, 2005, Caprotti et al., 2006), but its use was extended to spoken dialogue systems in the TALK project (Johansson 2006, Ljunglöf & al. 2006).

Let us rewrite the Sammie grammar fragment by using the library,

```
lincat
  Action     = Phr ; -- phrase
  ToIdentify = QS ;  -- question
  Object, Playlist,
    Artist   = NP ;  -- noun phrase
lin
  create = imperative (mkVP create_V2
    (indef (mkCN new_A playlist_N))) ;
  identify x = mkPhr x ;
  play x = imperative (mkVP play_V2 x) ;
  remove x y =
    imperative (mkVP remove_V3 y x);
  currently_playing_object =
    mkQS whatSg_IP (mkNP name_N2
      (mkNP this_Quant song_N)) ;
```

This grammar uses the language-independent resource grammar API with categories such as `Phr, QS, NP` and constructors such as `mkVP, indef, this_Quant`. The ones provided by the resource grammar are syntactic combination rules and structural words, which are independent of the domain of application.

In addition to the resource API elements, a concrete syntax also needs a lexicon of domain-specific words, such as `new_A, play_V2, remove_V3` above. The resource library provides for each language a set of operations for constructing lexical entries with all morphosyntactic information they need. Thus the three mentioned objects are defined as follows in English:

```
new_A = regA "new" ;
play_V2 = dirV2 (regV "play") ;
remove_V3 = dirV3
  (regV "remove") from_Prep ;
```

Here are the German definitions:

```
new_A = regA "neu" ;
play_V2 = dirV2 (regV "spielen") ;
remove_V3 = dirV3
  (prefixV "heraus" nehmen_V) aus_Prep ;
```

The lexicon definitions are gathered into a separate **interface** module, which the concrete syntax module depends on. All that is needed to add a new language to the system is a new implementation of the interface module, with lexical entries belonging to that language.

3.2 Beyond baseline grammars

A baseline multilingual grammar system can be obtained by defining the syntax in a language-independent way using the resource API, and only letting the lexical entries vary from one language to another. Such a system is guaranteed to be grammatically correct, as regards to word order and agreement. But the different languages often come out unidiomatic. For instance, the above rule for `currently_playing_object` produces the translations

```
vad är namnet på den här sången
was ist der name von diesem lied
quel est le nom de cette chanson
mikä on tämän laulun nimi
what is the name of this song
```

These translations are OK for Finnish and English, but very clumsy for the rest of the languages, which have special verbs for expressing the name of a subject (the proper forms were shown above; the closest corresponding English idiom is *what is this song called*).

Fortunately, GF is a functional programming language that permits functions, instead of just words, to appear in an interface. An improved way to implement the rule above is

```
lin currently_playing_object =
  mkQS (what_name
    (mkNP this_Quant song_N))
```

where the function `what_name` has different implementations in different languages: here, for instance, German and English:

```
what_name x =
  mkQCl how_IAdv (pred heißen_V x)
what_name x =
  mkQCl whatSg_IP (mkNP (regN2 "name") x)
```

A similar refinement is needed in the GF Sammie grammar to express imperatives. A baseline, language-independent definition would be

```
imperative vp = UttImpSg vp
```

which produces the second-person singular imperative form of a verb phrase. In German, as shown by the corpus collected for Sammie, both the familiar singular and the polite imperative are appropriate, and should be accepted in user input. GF has the `variants` construct to express such free variation:

```
imperative vp = variants {
  UttImpSg vp ;
  UttImpPol vp
  }
```

When extending the different languages of the Sammie grammar in GF, above the baseline, adding variants was the prominent method used.

3.3 Using GF in dialogue systems

In the TALK project, GF was used for building various components of dialogue systems at three different sites. The most relevant features of GF in this work were the following:

- a common abstract syntax guarantees that the same semantics is implemented for all languages
- the resource grammar library makes it easier to port systems to new languages
- the GF grammar compiler supports the production of many other formats from the GF source

The first two features have been covered in the preceding sections. The third feature, the grammar compiler, is what in practice can integrate GF in the work flow of different projects. Language models for speech recognition are the most crucial formats in dialogue systems. GF supports several such formats, including the GSL format used in the Nuance system, which in turn is used in the Sammie dialogue system. Porting the Sammie grammar to new languages with GF would thus automatically produce the required speech recognition grammars.

4 The first experiment

The starting point of the work was Nuance-Sammie, a pair of hand-written Nuance grammars used in the Sammie system, one for English (NuanceEng) and one for German (NuanceGer). The goal was to produce GF-Sammie, a GF grammar with the same coverage as Nuance-Sammie, but for more languages.

This was to be produced by using the resource grammar library, and share as much code as possible between the languages.

The experiment was aimed to test the hypotheses that a grammar for basic communication is easy to produce using the library; adding a new language should be a matter of a few hours.

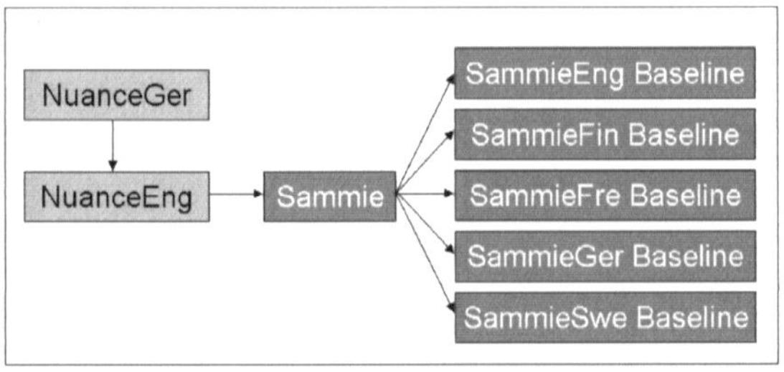

Figure 1: First experiment: The baseline grammar development. The modules on the left are handwritten Nuance grammars used in the Sammie system. The module in the middle is a GF abstract syntax defining the semantics implicit in the Nuance grammars. The modules on the right are GF concrete syntaxes implementing the semantics in a minimal but complete way.

4.1 The phases of the work

Before the baseline grammar, an abstract syntax must of course be produced. It was written by Björn Bringert on the basis of NuanceEng, which was richly commented with information indicating what actions should be covered by the grammar. The abstract syntax was produced in five hours, which includes the work needed to write a string-based English concrete syntax to test the abstract syntax.

To prepare for a multilingual localization, the string-based English concrete syntax was first **globalized** by rewriting it in terms of the recource grammar API and moving lexical items and some other obviously English-dependent constructs to an interface. This work took two hours.

After the globalization, the grammar was localized by writing new instances of the interface. This was done for Swedish, Finnish, French, and German. The work took half an hour for each language.

Did we now have a satisfactory baseline grammar for five languages? This was tested by generating sentences in all languages, and led to some fine-tuning to get satisfactory (grammatical and idiomatic) results. But now we did have a grammar that permitted user input in five languages, with the same semantics as NuanceEng, but with more limited variation in expressions. Spanish was added later to the system. Summary of the time consumption for this work is as follows:

- abstract syntax and string-based English: 5h
- globalized English by use of resource API: 2h
- five new languages: 5h

A baseline grammar, as we have defined it, covers the abstract syntax with a minimal, grammatically correct and stylistically acceptable concrete syntax. Such a grammar can be used for communication by users who are willing to learn to speak in a certain way. Notice that this can still be richer than a Command&Control system, because the dialogue manager is based on the language-independent abstract syntax and works quite as well with a minimal concrete syntax.

The next phase was to grow the coverage of one of the baseline grammars, SammieGer Baseline, to match the corpus defined by NuanceGer. This work was expected to take a few days, as carried out by a non-linguist programmer who first had to learn GF.

5 The second experiment

As expected, the SammieGer Baseline grammar covered less user utterances than the NuanceGer grammar. The purpose of our experiment was to find out how much time and effort a GF-novice grammar engineer needed to extend the SammieGer Baseline grammar to match the coverage of the NuanceGer grammar. The top level grammars involved can be seen in Figure 2.

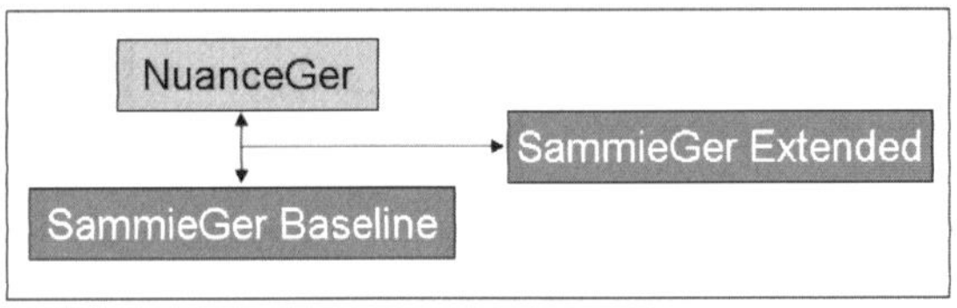

Figure 2: Second experiment: The SammieGer Baseline was extended to SammieGer Extended, to match the coverage of the original NuanceGer.

5.1 Experimental plan

For the extension of the SammieGer Baseline grammar, we were in the fortunate position of already having a grammar at hand that defined the terminal symbols and the grammar rules which the SammieGer Extended grammar would have to include. We planned the extension experiment in the following way: Comparing the coverage of SammieGer with the original NuanceGer grammar by generating sentences from the Nuance grammar and checking if they are covered by the GF grammar. If a generated sentence is grammatically correct but contains words that are missing in the lexicon, the GF lexicon has to be extended. If the syntactic structure is not covered, the concrete syntax has to be extended, and if the semantic structure of the sentence is missing in the abstract grammar, it has to be added.

5.2 Adding words to the lexicon

Before generating sentences from the NuanceGer grammar, we started with a simple word count. The NuanceGer grammar contained 463 single words, counting all inflected forms of the same stem individually. The SammieGer Baseline grammar contained 100 words, so it was clear that our first action had to be the extension of the SammieGer lexicon. Wherever this was possible using the **variants** construct (cf. Section 3.2), i.e. when adding a word that is a synonym of a word which was already modeled in the SammieGer grammar, this was most comfortable. 46 words could be added in this fashion, this time counting morphological infinitive forms that added more than one inflected form to the grammar. In fact, the 46 infinitive forms extended the word count to 215, so that the adding of 46 infinitives extended the grammar by 115 inflected word forms.

Some of these words had to be added because the starting point for the SammieGer Baseline grammar was in fact an English (NuanceEng) grammar. When translating from German to English, some words got lost, for instance, the words "Sänger" and "Sängerin" united to the word "singer" in English, as there is no gender distinction in English. The word "Sängerin" is missing in the SammieGer Baseline grammar, as "Sänger" only becomes translated to "singer".

Another source of words are verbs with their respective removable prefixes. German is rich in prefixes that can be combined with verbs to gain new meanings, for instance "an-gehen", "auf-gehen", "aus-gehen" [...], which are all related verbs sharing word stem and inflection paradigms, but each mean something else. These prefixes can be severed from the verb in certain utterances, and fortunately, GF accounts for that. By extending play_V (cmp. above) to:

```
play_V2 = variants {
  dirV2 (regV "spielen") ;
  dirV2 (prefixV "ab" (regV "spielen"))
  } ;
```

the extended grammar is able to parse an utterance like "spiele einen Titel von U2 ab" ("play a title by U2"), as well as an utterance without the "ab" in the end. The linearization rules in GF place the severed prefix in the syntactically correct position.

There were also words missing from the SammieGer Baseline grammar that could not be included with a simple variants construct. They were added to the lexicon under new identifiers and integrated into the concrete grammar by writing new linearization rules. In order to accomodate some of the missing words, new abstract syntax rules had to be defined.

5.3 Adding rules to the concrete grammar

One example of additions to the concrete syntax are the rules for interrogative and infinitive forms. Utterances follow certain patterns which are also reflected in the NuanceGer grammar (see Table 1 for an overview). In the Baseline SammieGer, only the imperative construct was modeled. The detour we took in localizing the system over English accounts for one missing utterance type: the infinitive and the imperative type are identical in English, but not in German. The interrogative forms are phrased like questions, but contain an implicit but politely expressed imperative. We managed to include the other utterance types by adding four rules to the concrete SammieGer grammar and renaming rule identifiers in one referenced library grammar.

5.4 Adding rules to the abstract grammar

Some user intentions modeled in the NuanceGer grammar were missing in the abstract SammieGer Baseline grammar, for instance scrolling a list presented on the screen up or down. These additions

Table 1: *Utterances Types.* The types of user utterances for German and English. Note that the imperative and the infitive forms in are the same in English, but not in German.

Type	German Example	English Example
Imperative	Spiele Vertigo von U2.	Play Vertigo by U2.
Interrogative	Kannst du Vertigo von U2 spielen?	Can you play Vertigo by U2?
Indicative	Ich möchte Vertigo von U2 hören.	I want to listen to Vertigo by U2.
Infinitive	Vertigo von U2 spielen.	Play Vertigo by U2.

took one day to accomplish. Summary of the time needed for the grammar extension is as follows:

- Installing and learning GF: 4 days
- Adding words: 3 days
- Adding concrete syntax rules: 3 days
- Adding abstract syntax rules: 1 day

6 Results

In this section, we compare the SammieGer Baseline/Extended and the NuanceGer grammar.

The goal set for the first experiment to build prototypical grammars for six languages was fulfilled quite successfully. However, the aim of the second experiment to match the coverage of the NuanceGer grammar with the SammieGer Extended grammar was not reached as quickly as we had hoped. It took a substantial time for the programmer to learn GF well, and the the development cycle was slowed down by fairly long compilation times. The resource library was difficult to navigate and contained some bugs that were fixed during the experiment, which caused waiting time. Nevertheless, the SammieGer Extended grammar's coverage increased considerably compared to SammieGer Baseline. Moreover, most of the extensions made to the German grammar can be ported to the other languages with very little work, due to the common resource library API.

6.1 Statistics

The original German grammar NuanceGer was written in approximately 18 days. In the GF experiments, 12 hours were needed to create the six baseline grammars from the NuanceEng original, and about 7 days for the SammieGer Extended grammar (not counting the time needed for installation and learning to use GF). If we sum up the SammieGer Baseline and the SammieGer Extended grammar writing time, we end up with 8 days for the SammieGer combined. This is faster than the 18 days spent on the original NuanceGer grammar, but we had of course the advantage of already having NuanceGer available: its authors had to start from scratch and continuously add words and rules after user evaluations. Moreover, the full coverage of NuanceGer was not reached, mostly because of colloquial forms of speech that were not covered by the resource library. Statistics of the coverage of the three grammars (SammieGer Baseline, SammieGer Extended, and NuanceGer) can be seen in Table 2.

6.2 Related work

The idea of generating speech recognition grammars from higher-level formats was first implemented in the Regulus system (Rayner et al., 2006). The source format of Regulus is a unification-based grammar formalism, and the target is GSL (the format used in Nuance); GF supports many other formats as well, such as the SLF format used in HTK (Young et al., 2005); see (Bringert, 2007). Regulus also has a resource grammar library currently covering five languages.

GF was previously used for dialogue system localization in the TALK project, where seven languages were covered (Johansson, 2006, Ljunglöf et al., 2006).

6.3 Conclusion

GF provides elegant solutions for many grammar writing challenges. Based on the concept of one abstract and many concrete grammars for different languages, GF is well-suited for localization tasks and fast prototyping in multiple languages. One disadvantage of GF is that it is quite difficult to get a grasp

Table 2: Statistics of SammieGer Baseline, SammieGer Extended, and the original Nuance.

Grammar	Baseline	Extended	Original
top-level constructors	18	23	~23
syntactic categories	17	17	419
German - specific source code	4kB	18kB	200kB
German + generic source code	14kB	33kB	200kB
Nuance code	18kB	31kB	200kB
distinct words	100	325	463

of the framework quickly, compared to the concept of a context free grammar format in BNF or EBNF form which is easier to understand, for computer scientists as well as for linguists. As GF is more of a programming language than a grammar format, it implements much more constructs than BNF, which also makes it more powerful. That power can be seen in the comparison of source code size between NuanceGer and SammieGer Extended in Table 2.

The elegance of the many resource files that hide the complexity leads to difficulties in error detection, as there is a tree of resource grammars referencing other grammars and to the novice programmer, it is not always transparent where an error occurred. This is of course a problem with all high-level programming languages using libraries. A more intuitive IDE and faster compilation times could improve the system's usability significantly.

Grammatically correct utterances can be modeled nicely in the GF resource grammar library, which also eliminated some of the grammatical errors present in the original hand-coded Nuance grammar. However, some spoken language oriented rules were not covered by the library, and were implemented by brute force by using strings in GF. In this experiment, the resource grammar was taken as it was (apart from bug fixes), and no new functions were added to it.

References

T. Becker, N. Blaylock, C. Gerstenberger, A. Korthauer, N. Perera, M. Pitz, P. Poller, J. Schehl, F. Steffens, R. Stegmann, and J. Steigner (Editor). 2007. *TALK Deliverable D5.3: In-Car Showcase Based on TALK Libraries.*

B. Bringert. 2007. *Speech Recognition Grammar Compilation in Grammatical Framework.* SPEECHGRAM 2007, Prague, 29 June 2007.

D. Burke and K. Johannisson. 2005. *Translating Formal Software Specifications to Natural Language / A Grammar-Based Approach.* P. Blache, E. Stabler, J. Busquets and R. Moot (eds). *Logical Aspects of Computational Linguistics (LACL 2005).* LNCS/LNAI 3407, pages 51–66.

O. Caprotti. 2007. *WebALT! Deliver Mathematics Everywhere.* Proceedings of SITE 2006. Orlando March 20-24.

E. Hagen, T. Said, and J. Eckert. 2004. *Spracheingabe im neuen BMW 6er.* ATZ.

R. Haller. 2003. *The Display and Control Concept iDrive - Quick Access to All Driving and Comfort Functions.* ATZ/MTZ Extra (The New BMW 5-Series), pages 51–53.

A. Ranta. 2004. *Grammatical Framework: A type-theoretical grammar formalism.* Journal of Functional Programming,14(2):145–189.

M. Johansson. 2006. *Globalization and Localization of a Dialogue System using a Resource Grammar.* Master's thesis, Göteborg University.

P. Ljunglöf, G. Amores, R. Cooper, D. Hjelm, O. Lemon, P. Manchón, G. Pérez, and A. Ranta. 2006. *Multimodal Grammar Library.* TALK Talk and Look: Tools for Ambient Linguistic Knowledge IST-507802 Deliverable 1.2b

M. Rayner, P. Bouillon, B. A. Hockey, and N. Chatzichrisafis. 2006. *REGULUS: A Generic Multilingual Open Source Platform for Grammar-Based Speech Applications.* In Proceedings of LREC, 24-26 May 2006, Genoa, Italy.

S. Young, G. Evermann, M. Gales, T. Hain, D. Kershaw, G. Moore, J. Odell., D. Ollason, D. Povey, V. Valtchev, and P. Woodland. 2005. *The HTK Book (for HTK Version 3.3).* Cambridge University Engineering Department.

Grammar-based context-specific statistical language modelling

Rebecca Jonson
Department of Linguistics, Göteborg University & GSLT
Box 200, 40530 Göteborg, Sweden
rj@ling.gu.se

Abstract

This paper shows how we can combine the art of grammar writing with the power of statistics by bootstrapping statistical language models (SLMs) for Dialogue Systems from grammars written using the Grammatical Framework (GF) (Ranta, 2004). Furthermore, to take into account that the probability of a user's dialogue moves is not static during a dialogue we show how the same methodology can be used to generate dialogue move specific SLMs where certain dialogue moves are more probable than others. These models can be used at different points of a dialogue depending on contextual constraints. By using grammar generated SLMs we can improve both recognition and understanding performance considerably over using the original grammar. With dialogue move specific SLMs we would be able to get a further improvement if we had an optimal way of predicting the correct language model.

1 Introduction

Speech recognition (ASR) for dialogue systems is often caught in the trap of the sparse data problem which excludes the possibility of using statistical language models (SLMs). A common approach is to write a grammar for the domain either as a speech recognition grammar (SRG) or as an interpretation grammar which can be compiled into a speech recognition grammar (SRG) using some grammar development platform such as Gemini, Regulus or GF (Rayner et al., 2000; Rayner et al., 2006; Ranta, 2004). The last option will assure that the linguistic coverage of the ASR and interpretation are kept in sync. ASR for commercial dialogue systems has mainly focused on grammar-based approaches despite the fact that SLMs seem to have a better overall performance (Knight et al., 2001; Bangalore and Johnston, 2003). This probably depends on the time-consuming work of collecting corpora for training SLMs compared with the more rapid and straightforward development of SRGs. However, SLMs are more robust for out-of-coverage input, perform better in difficult conditions and seem to work better for naive users as shown in (Knight et al., 2001). SRGs on the other hand are limited in their coverage depending on how well grammar writers succeed in predicting what users may say.

An approach taken in both dialogue systems and dictation applications is to write a grammar for the particular domain and generate an artificial corpus from the grammar to be used as training corpus for SLMs (Galescu et al., 1998; Bangalore and Johnston, 2003; Jonson, 2006). These grammar-based models are not as accurate as the ones built from real data as the estimates are artificial, lacking a realistic distribution. However, as has been shown in (Bangalore and Johnston, 2003; Jonson, 2006) these grammar-based statistical models seem to have a much more robust behaviour than their corresponding grammars which leaves us with a much better starting point in the first development stage in a dialogue system. It is a way of compromising between the ease of grammar writing and the robust-

Proceedings of SPEECHGRAM 2007, pages 25–32,
Prague, Czech Republic, June 2007.

ness of SLMs. With this methodology we can use the knowledge and intuition we have about the domain and include it in our first SLM and get a much more robust behaviour than with a grammar. From this starting point we can then collect more data with our first prototype of the system to improve our SLM. In this paper the advantage of this method is shown further by evaluating a different domain in greater detail.

Context-specific models have shown important recognition performance gain (Baggia et al., 1997; Riccardi et al., 1998; Xu and Rudnicky, 2000; Lemon and Gruenstein, 2004) and have usually been of two types: created as state-specific grammars or built from collected data partitioned according to dialogue states. Both methods have their disadvantages. In the first case, we constrain the user heavily which makes them unsuitable for use in a more flexible system such as an information-state based system. This can be solved by having a back-off method but leaves us with extra processing (Lemon and Gruenstein, 2004). In the latter case, we have an even more severe sparse data problem than when creating a general SLM as we need enough data to get a good distribution of data over dialogue states. In an information-state based system where the user is not restricted to only a few dialogue states this problem gets even worse. In addition, why we chose to work with grammar-based SLMs in the first place was because data is seldom available in the first stage of dialogue system development. This leaves us with the requirement of an SLM that although being context-specific does not constrain the user and which assures a minimal coverage of expressions for a certain context. In (Gruenstein et al., 2005) this is accomplished by dynamically populating a class-based SLMs with context-sensitive content words and utterances. In this paper, we will show how we can use the same methodology as in (Jonson, 2006) to create context-specific SLMs from grammars based on dialogue moves that match these criteria.

This study is organized as follows. First, we introduce our methodology for developing SLMs from grammars. Section 3 describes the data collection of test utterances and how we have partitioned the data into different test sets depending on grammar coverage, types of users and types of dialogue moves. In section 4, we show and discuss the results of the different models for different test sets and finally we draw some conclusions from the experiments.

2 Grammar-based SLMs

In (Jonson, 2006) we described how we could generate an SLM from an interpretation grammar written in GF for an MP3 player application and get a much more robust behaviour than by using the original grammar for ASR. In this study, we approach a different domain using a GF grammar written for a dialogue system application called AgendaTalk (Ericsson et al., 2006). It is one of several applications that has been developed in the TALK project (www.talk-project.org) and has been built with the TrindiKit toolkit and the GoDiS dialogue system (Larsson, 2002) as a GoDiS application. It works as a voice interface to a graphical calendar. Apart from evaluating a different domain in a more extensive way to see if the tendency we found in (Jonson, 2006) is consisting over domains, we have driven the methodology a bit further to be able to generate context-specific SLMs that favour certain parts of the grammar, in our case certain dialogue moves. We call these SLMs "dialogue move specific SLMs" (DMSLMs). Both types of models are obtained by generating all possible utterances from a GF grammar, building trigram SLMs from the grammar-based corpus using the SRI language modelling toolkit (Stolcke, 2002) and compiling them into recognition packages. For comparison we have also compiled the GF grammar directly into a Nuance speech recognition grammar using the GF compiler.

2.1 Building a general SLM from grammar-based corpora

The GF grammar written for the calendar domain consists of 500 GF functions (rules) where 220 are domain-specific and 280 inherited from a domain-independent grammar. It exists in two equivalent language versions that share the same GF functions: English and Swedish. We have used GF's facilities to generate a corpus from the Swedish version consisting of all possible meaningful utterances generated by the grammar to a certain depth of the analysis trees in GF's abstract syntax. The grammar is written on the phrase level accepting spoken language utterances such as e.g. "add a booking please". The resulting corpus consists of 1.7 million utterances and 19 million words with a vocabulary of only 183 words. All utterances in the corpus occur exactly once. However, all grammar rules are not expanded which leaves us with a class-tagged corpus without e.g. all variants of date expressions but with the class `date`. What we get in the end is therefore a class-based SLM that we compile into a recognition package together with a rule-based description of these classes. The SLM has 3 different classes: `time`, `date` and `event` and the domain vocabulary when including all distinct words in these classes make up almost 500 words.

Adding real speech corpora

In (Jonson, 2006) we saw that the use of real corpora in interpolation with our artificial corpus was only valuable as long as the real corpora approximated the language of use. The big news corpus we had available did not give any significant improvement but the transcribed Swedish speech corpus we used was much more helpful. In this study we have therefore once again used the GLSC corpus to improve our word occurrence estimates by interpolating it with our grammar-based SLM. The Gothenburg Spoken Language (GSLC) corpus consists of transcribed Swedish spoken language from different social activities such as auctions, phone calls, meetings, lectures and task-oriented dialogue (Allwood, 1999). The corpus is composed of about 1,300,000 words and is turn-based which gives it long utterances including e.g. transcribed disfluencies. From this corpus we have built an SLM which we have interpolated with our grammar-based SLM keeping our domain vocabulary. This means we are just considering those n-grams in the GSLC corpus which match the domain vocabulary to hopefully get a more realistic probability distribution for these. We will call this model our `Extended SLM`.

2.2 Dialogue move specific SLMs

SLMs capture the lexical context statistics in a specific language use. However, the statistical distribution in a dialogue is not static but varies by boosting and lowering probabilities for different words and expressions depending on contextual appropriateness. It is not only words and expressions that vary their distribution but on a semantic level different conceptual messages will be more or less probable as a user utterance at different points of the dialogue. This means that certain dialogue moves will have a higher degree of expectancy at a specific point of the dialogue. To capture this phenomenon, we want to build models that raise the probability of certain dialogue moves in certain contexts by giving a higher probability for utterances expressing these dialogue moves. These are models where utterances corresponding to a certain dialogue move are more salient (e.g. a model where all ways of answering yes or no are more plausible than other utterances). Such a model will account for the fact that the expectation of dialogue moves a user will perform varies in a dialogue and thereby their statistics. We can obtain this by using a version of the grammar-based corpus where the dialogue moves for each utterance are generated which allows us to partition the corpus in different ways based on dialogue moves. We can then take out part of the corpus e.g. all utterances corresponding to a certain dialogue move, create an SLM and interpolate it with the general grammar-based SLM. In this way, we get SLMs where certain dialogue moves are more probable than others and where minimally all possible expressions for these, which the grammar describes, are covered. By interpolating with the general SLM we put no hard constraints on the expected dialogue move so the user can in fact say anything at any point in the dialogue despite the raised expectancy for certain dialogue moves. We just boost the expected probability of certain dialogue moves and their possible expressions. By using contextual constraints in the information state we could then predict which model to use and switch SLMs on the fly so that we obtain a recognizer that takes account of expected user input.

2.2.1 Partitioning the training data by dialogue moves

In GoDiS, dialogue moves are activity related and exist in seven different types: `request` moves, `answer` moves, `ask` moves (i.e. questions), yes and no (`yn`) answers, `greet` moves, `quit` moves and feedback and sequencing moves which are called `ICM:s` (Larsson, 2002). We have chosen to focus on the first four of these dialogue move types to build up our DMSLMs. We have used GF to generate a corpus with all possible dialogue moves and their combinations with their corresponding expressions. From this corpus we have extracted all utterances that can be interpreted as an `answer` move or a sequence of answer moves, all expressions for specification of a `request` (in GoDiS what type of action to perform e.g. deleting a booking), all ways of expressing questions in our grammars (i.e. `ask` moves) and all possible `yn` answers. This leaves us with four new sets of training data.

The decision to partition the data in this way was based on the distribution of dialogue moves in our data where the moves we focus on are the most common ones and the most critical for achievement of the dialogue tasks. As these dialogue moves are abstract and domain-independent it would be possible to use a domain-independent prediction of these dialogue moves and thereby the language models although the structure of the SLMs would be different in different domains.

2.2.2 Building dialogue move specific SLMs

For each set of dialogue move specific training data we created an SLM that only captures ways of expressing a specific dialogue move. However, we are looking for less constrained models which just alter the probability of certain dialogue moves. By interpolating the SLMs built on dialogue move specific corpora with the general grammar-based SLM we achieve models with contextual probabilities but that generalize to avoid constraining the user input.

The interpolation of these models was carried out with the SRILM toolkit based on equation 1. The optimal lambda weight was estimated to 0.85 for all models with the SRILM toolkit using held-out data.

$$P_{dmslm}(W) = \lambda P_{movespec}(W) + (1 - \lambda)P_{general}(W) \quad (1)$$

We ended up with four new SLMs, so called DM-SLMs, in which either the probability of `answer`, `ask`, `request` or `yn` moves were boosted.

3 Test Data

The collection of test data was carried out by having people interacting with the AgendaTalk system using the grammar-based SLM. The test group included both naive users with no experience of the system whatsoever and users that had previous experience with the system to varying extents. We have classified the latter group as expert users although the expertise varies considerably. All users were given a printed copy of a calendar month with scheduled bookings and some question marks and were assigned the task of altering the voice-based calendar so that the graphical calendar would look the same as the printed copy except for the question marks which they were to find values for by querying the system. This would mean that they would have to add, delete and alter bookings as well as find out information about their schedule e.g. the time of an event. The tasks could be carried out in any order and there were many different ways to complete the schedule.

The data collection gave us a recording test set of 1000 recorded utterances from 15 persons (all native, 8 female, 7 male). This unrestricted test set was used to compare recognition performance between the different models under consideration. We also partitioned the test set in various ways to explore different features. The test set was parsed to get all in-coverage utterances that the original GF grammar covers to create an in-coverage test set from these. In addition, we partitioned the data by users with a test set with the naive user utterances and another test set from the expert users. In this way we could explore how our models performed under different conditions. Different dialogue system applications will have a different distribution of users. Some systems will always have a large number of naive or less experienced users who will use more out-of-coverage utterances and more out-of-vocabulary (OOV) words whereas users of other applications will have the opportunity to obtain considerable experience which will allow them to adapt to the system, in particular to its grammar and vocabulary.

The recordings for the unrestricted test set have an OOV rate of 6% when using our domain vocabulary. The naive test set makes up 529 of these recordings with an OOV rate of 8% whereas the expert test set of 471 recordings has a lower OOV rate of 4%. The in-coverage test set consists of 626 utterances leaving us with an in-coverage rate of 62.6% for the unrestricted test set. This shows the need for a more robust way of recognition and interpretation if we expect to expose the system to less experienced users.

For the evaluation of the DMSLMs we have partitioned the test data by dialogue moves. The utterances corresponding with the four dialogue moves chosen for our DMSLMs were divided into four test sets. The utterances left were used to create a fifth test set where none of our four DMSLMs would apply but where we would need to use the general model. If we look at the distribution of the test data considering dialogue moves we find that 75.4% of the test data falls into our four dialogue move categories and that only 24.6% of the data would require the general model. This part of the test data includes dialogue moves such as greetings, quit moves and dialogue move sequences with combinations of different moves. The most common dialogue move in our data is an `answer` move or a sequence of `answer` moves resulting in common utterances such as: "a meeting on friday" as answer to system questions such as "what booking do you want to add?".

4 Experimental Results

To evaluate the recognition performance of our different types of models we ran several experiments on the different test sets. We report results on word error rate (WER), sentence error rate (SER) and also on a semantic level by reporting what we call dialogue move error rate (DMER). The dialogue move error rate was obtained by parsing the recognized utterances and comparing these to a parsed version of the transcriptions, calculating the rate of correctly parsed dialogue moves. The calculation was done in the same way as calculation of concept error rate (CER) proposed by (Boros et al., 1996) where the degree of correctly recognized concepts is considered. In our case this means the degree of correctly recognized dialogue moves. For parsing we have used a phrase-spotting grammar written in Prolog that pattern matches phrases to dialogue moves. Using the original GF interpretation grammar for parsing would have restricted us to the coverage of the grammar which is not an optimal choice together with SLMs. Ideally, we would like to use a robust version of GF to be able to use the original GF grammar both for parsing and SLM generation and by that assure the same linguistic coverage. Attempts to do this have been carried out in the TALK project for the MP3 domain by training a dialogue move tagger on the same type of corpus that was used for the DMSLMs where dialogue moves occur together with their corresponding utterances. Other methods of relaxing the constraints of the GF parser are also under consideration. Meanwhile, we are using a simple robust phrase spotting parser. We have investigated both how our grammar-based SLMs perform in comparison to our grammar under different conditions to see how recognition and understanding performance varies as well as how our DMSLMs perform in comparison to the general grammar-based SLM. The results are reported in the following sections. All models have the same domain vocabulary and the OOV figures presented earlier thereby apply for all of them.

4.1 Grammar-based SLMs vs. grammars

Table 1 shows the results for our different language models on our unrestricted test set of 1000 utterances as well as for the part of this test set which is in-coverage. As expected they all perform much better on the in-coverage test set with the lowest WER obtained with our grammar. On the unrestricted test set we can see an important reduction of both WER (26% and 38% relative improvement) and DMER (24% and 40% relative improvement) for the SLMs in comparison to the grammar which indicates the robustness of these to new user input.

In table 2 we can see how the performance of all our models are better for the expert users with a relative word error rate reduction from 25% to 32% in comparison to the results for the naive test set. The same pattern is seen on the semantic level with important reduction in DMER. The result is expected as the expert users have greater knowledge of the language of the system. This is consistent with the results reported in (Knight et al., 2001). It is also reflected in the OOV figures discussed earlier where the naive users seem to have used many more unknown words than the expert users.

This shows that the models perform very differently depending on the types of users and how much they hold to the coverage of the grammar. Our grammar-based SLM gives us a much more robust behaviour which is good when we expect less experienced users. However, we can see that we get a degradation in in-coverage performance which would be critical if we are to use the model in a system where we expect that the users will achieve cer-

Table 1: *Results on unrestricted vs in-coverage test set*

Model	Unrestricted			In-coverage		
	WER	SER	DMER	WER	SER	DMER
Grammar	39.0%	47.6%	43.2%	10.7%	16.3%	10.3%
Grammar-based SLM	29.0%	39.7%	33.0%	14.8%	18.3%	13.7%
Extended SLM	24.0%	35.2%	25.8%	11.5%	15.8%	10.4%

Table 2: *Results on naive vs expert users*

Model	Naive users			Expert users		
	WER	SER	DMER	WER	SER	DMER
Grammar	46.6%	50.3%	54.7%	31.7%	44.4%	33.2%
Grammar-based SLM	34.4%	42.9%	41.3%	23.8%	35.9%	25.8%
Extended SLM	27.6%	38.2%	29.5%	20.7%	31.8%	22.7%

tain proficiency. The `Extended SLM` seem to perform well in all situations and if we look at DMER there is no significant difference in performance between this model and our grammar when it comes to in-coverage input. In most systems we will probably have a range of users with different amounts of experience and even experienced users will fail to follow the grammar in spontaneous speech. This points towards the advisability of using an SLM as it is more robust and if it does not degrade too much on in-coverage user input like the `Extended SLM` it would be an optimal choice.

From the results it seems that we have found a correlation between the DMER and WER in our system which indicates that if we manage to lower WER we will also achieve better understanding performance with our simple robust parser. This is good news as it means that we will not only capture more words with our SLMs but also more of the message the user is trying to convey in the sense of capturing more dialogue moves. This will definitely result into a better dialogue system performance overall. Interestingly, we have been able to obtain this just by converting our grammar into an SLM.

4.2 Dialogue move specific SLMs vs General SLMs

We have evaluated our DMSLMs on test sets for each model which include only utterances that correspond to the dialogue moves in the model. It should be mentioned that the test sets may include utterances not covered by the original GF grammar e.g. a different wording for the same move. The results for each DMSLM on its specific test set and the performance of the grammar-based SLM and the Extended SLM are reported in tables 3, 4, 5 and 6.

Table 3: *Ask Move SLM*

Model	WER	SER	DMER
Grammar-based SLM	39.2%	68.4%	51.8%
Ask DMSLM	31.8%	68.9%	48.7%
Extended SLM	30.1%	58.0%	44.6%

Table 4: *Answer Move SLM*

Model	WER	SER	DMER
Grammar-based SLM	17.3%	22.0%	16.3%
Answer DMSLM	15.7%	20.1%	14.1%
Extended SLM	18.2%	22.0%	16.7%

Table 5: *Request Move SLM*

Model	WER	SER	DMER
Grammar-based SLM	29.1%	44.3%	27.0%
Request DMSLM	17.0%	36.1%	14.7%
Extended SLM	26.3%	42.6%	22.1%

Apart from these four dialogue moves our test data includes a lot of different dialogue moves and dialogue move combinations that we have not considered. As we have no specific model for these we would need to use a general model in these cases. This means that apart from predicting the four dialogue moves we have considered we would also need to predict when none of these are expected and use the general model for these situations. In table 7 we can see how our general models perform on the rest of the test set. This shows that they seem to handle this part of the test data quite well.

Table 6: *YN Move SLM*

Model	WER	SER	DMER
Grammar-based SLM	37.3%	27.3%	22.7%
YN DMSLM	21.5%	16.5%	11.9%
Extended SLM	25.0%	18.2%	12.5%

Table 7: *General SLM on rest of test data*

Model	WER	SER	DMER
Grammar-based SLM	22.2%	42.7%	31.7%
Extended SLM	19.6%	39.8%	26.0%

We can see that the gain we get in recognition performance varies for the different models and that relative improvement in WER goes from 9% for the `answer` model to 42% for our DMSLMs on appropriate test sets. We can see that our models have most problems with `ask` moves and `yn` answers. In the case of `ask` moves this seems to be because our GF grammar is missing a lot of syntactic constructions of question expressions. This would then explain why the Extended SLM gets a much better figure here. The GSLC corpus does capture more of this expressive variation of questions. In other words we seem to have failed to capture and predict the linguistic usage with our hand-tailored grammar. In the case of `yn` answers the result reveals that our grammar-based SLM does not have a realistic distribution of these expressions at all. This seems to be something the GSLC corpus contribute, considering the good results for the `Extended SLM`. However, we can see that we can achieve the same effect by boosting the probability of yes and no answers in our DMSLM.

If we look at the overall achievement in recognition performance, using our DMSLMs when appropriate and in other cases the general SLM, the average WER of 22% (27% DMER) is considerably lower than when using the general model for the same test data (29% WER, 33% DMER). If we had an optimal method for predicting what language model to use we would be able to decrease WER by 24% relative. If we chose to use the `Extended SLM` in the cases our DMSLMs do not cover we could get an even greater reduction.

We have also tested how well our DMSLMs perform on the general test set (i.e. all 1000 utterances) to see how bad the performance would be if we chose the wrong model. In table 8 we can see that this approach yields an average WER of 30% which is a minimal degradation in comparison to the general grammar-based SLM. On the contrary, some of our models actually perform better than our general grammar-based SLM or very similarly. This implies that there is no substantial risk on recognition performance if our prediction model would fail. This means that we could obtain very good results with important recognition improvement even with an imperfect prediction accuracy. We have a relative improvement of 24% to gain with only a minimal loss.

Table 8: *DMSLMs on general test set*

Model	WER	SER
Answer DMSLM	34.7%	55.6%
Ask DMSLM	28.2%	46.2%
Request DMSLM	26.5%	43.2%
YN DMSLM	29.8%	44.0%

5 Concluding remarks

Our experimental results show that grammar-based SLMs give an important reduction in both WER and DMER in accordance with the results in (Jonson, 2006). We reach a relative improvement of 26% and a further 17% if we interpolate our grammar-based SLM with real speech data. The correlation of the DMER and the WER in our results indicates that the improved recognition performance will also propagate to the understanding performance of our system.

Context-specific language models (statistical and rule-based) have shown important recognition performance gain in earlier work (Baggia et al., 1997; Xu and Rudnicky, 2000; Lemon and Gruenstein, 2004; Gruenstein et al., 2005) and this study reaffirms that taking into account statistical language variation during a dialogue will give us more accurate recognition. The method we use here has the advantage that we can build statistical context-specific models even when no data is available, assuring a minimal coverage and by interpolation with a general model do not constrain the user input unduly.

The language model switch will be triggered by changing a variable in our information state: the predicted dialogue move. However, to be able to choose which language model suits the current information state best we need a way to predict dialogue moves. The prediction model could either be rule-based or data based. Our first experimental tests with machine learning for dialogue move prediction seems promising and we hope to report on these soon. Optimally, we want a prediction model that we can use in different GoDiS domains to be able to generate new DMSLMs from our domain-specific GF grammar for the dialogue moves we have considered here.

Our experiments show that we could achieve an overall reduction in WER of 46% and 40% in DMER if we were able to choose our best suited SLM instead of our compiled GF grammar. Naturally, we would have to take into account dialogue move prediction accuracy to get a more realistic figure. However, our experiments also show that the effect on performance if we failed to use the correct model would not be too harmful. This means we have much more to gain than to lose even if the dialogue move prediction is not perfect. This makes this approach a very interesting option in dialogue system development.

Acknowledgment

I would like to thank Nuance Communications Inc. for making available the speech recognition software used in this work.

References

Jens Allwood. 1999. The Swedish spoken language corpus at Göteborg University. In *Proceedings of Fonetik'99: The Swedish Phonetics Conference*.

Paolo Baggia, Morena Danieli, Elisabetta Gerbino, Loreta Moisa, and Cosmin Popovici. 1997. Contextual information and specific language models for spoken language understanding. In *Proceedings of SPECOM*.

Srinivas Bangalore and Michael Johnston. 2003. Balancing data-driven and rule-based approaches in the context of a multimodal conversational system. In *Proceedings of the ASRU Conference*.

M. Boros, W. Eckert, F. Gallwitz, G. Görz, G. Hanrieder, and H. Niemann. 1996. Towards understanding spontaneous speech: Word accuracy vs. concept accuracy. In *Proceedings of ICSLP*, Philadelphia, PA.

S. Ericsson, G. Amores, B. Bringert, H. Burden, A. Forslund, D. Hjelm, R. Jonson, S. Larsson, P. Ljunglöf, P. Manchon, D. Milward, G. Perez, and M. Sandin. 2006. Software illustrating a unified approach to multimodality and multilinguality in the in-home domain. Deliverable D1.6, TALK Project.

Lucian Galescu, Eric Ringger, and James Allen. 1998. Rapid language model development for new task domains. In *In Proceedings of the ELRA First International Conference on Language Resources and Evaluation (LREC)*.

Alexander Gruenstein, Chao Wang, and Stephanie Seneff. 2005. Context-sensitive statistical language modeling. In *Proceedings of Interspeech*.

Rebecca Jonson. 2006. Generating statistical language models from interpretation grammars in dialogue systems. In *Proceedings of EACL*, Trento, Italy.

S. Knight, G. Gorrell, M. Rayner, D. Milward, R. Koeling, and I. Lewin. 2001. Comparing grammar-based and robust approaches to speech understanding: A case study. In *Proceedings of Eurospeech*.

Staffan Larsson. 2002. *Issue-based Dialogue Management*. Ph.D. thesis, Göteborg University.

Oliver Lemon and Alexander Gruenstein. 2004. Multithreaded context for robust conversational interfaces: Context-sensitive speech recognition and interpretation of corrective fragments. *ACM Trans. Comput.-Hum. Interact.*, 11(3):241–267.

Aarne Ranta. 2004. Grammatical framework. a type-theoretical grammar formalism. *The Journal of Functional Programming*, 14(2):145–189.

Manny Rayner, Beth Ann Hockey, Frankie James, Elizabeth Owen Bratt, Sharon Goldwater, and Jean Mark Gawron. 2000. Compiling language models from a linguistically motivated unification grammar. In *Proceedings of the COLING*.

Manny Rayner, Beth Ann Hockey, and Pierrette Bouillon. 2006. *Putting Linguistics into Speech Recognition: The Regulus Grammar Compiler*. CSLI Publications.

Guiseppe Riccardi, Alexandros Potamianos, and Shrikanth Narayanan. 1998. Language model adaptation for spoken language systems. In *Proceedings of the ICSLP*, Australia.

Andreas Stolcke. 2002. SRILM - An extensible language modeling toolkit. In *Proceedings of ICSLP*, Denver, Colorado.

Wei Xu and Alex Rudnicky. 2000. Language modeling for dialog system. In *Proceedings of ICSLP 2000*, Beijing, China.

Handling Out-of-Grammar Commands in Mobile Speech Interaction Using Backoff Filler Models

Tim Paek[1], Sudeep Gandhe[2], David Maxwell Chickering[1], Yun Cheng Ju[1]
[1] Microsoft Research, One Microsoft Way, Redmond, WA 98052 USA
[2] USC Institute for Creative Technologies, 13274 Fiji Way, Marina del Rey, CA 90292, USA
{timpaek|dmax|yuncj}@microsoft.com, gandhe@usc.edu

Abstract

In command and control (C&C) speech interaction, users interact by speaking commands or asking questions typically specified in a context-free grammar (CFG). Unfortunately, users often produce out-of-grammar (OOG) commands, which can result in misunderstanding or non-understanding. We explore a simple approach to handling OOG commands that involves generating a backoff grammar from any CFG using filler models, and utilizing that grammar for recognition whenever the CFG fails. Working within the memory footprint requirements of a mobile C&C product, applying the approach yielded a 35% relative reduction in semantic error rate for OOG commands. It also improved partial recognitions for enabling clarification dialogue.

1 Introduction

In command and control (C&C) speech interaction, users interact with a system by speaking commands or asking questions. By defining a rigid syntax of possible phrases, C&C reduces the complexity of having to recognize unconstrained natural language. As such, it generally affords higher recognition accuracy, though at the cost of requiring users to learn the syntax of the interaction (Rosenfeld et al., 2001). To lessen the burden on users, C&C grammars are authored in an iterative fashion so as to broaden the coverage of likely expressions for commands, while remaining relatively simple for faster performance. Nevertheless, users can, and often still do, produce OOG commands. They may neglect to read the instructions, or forget the valid expressions. They may mistakenly believe that recognition is more robust than it really is, or take too long to articulate the right words. Whatever the reason, OOG commands can engender misunderstanding (i.e., recognition of the wrong command) or non-understanding (i.e., no recognition), and aggravate users who otherwise might not realize that their commands were OOG.

In this paper, we explore a simple approach to handling OOG commands, designed specifically to meet the memory footprint requirements of a C&C product for mobile devices. This paper is divided into three sections. First, we provide background on the C&C product and discuss the different types of OOG commands that occur with personal mobile devices. Second, we explain the details of the approach and how we applied it to the product domain. Finally, we evaluate the approach on data collected from real users, and discuss possible drawbacks.

2 Mobile C&C

With the introduction of voice dialing on mobile devices, C&C speech interaction hit the wider consumer market, albeit with rudimentary pattern recognition. Although C&C has been commonplace in telephony and accessibility for many years, only recently have mobile devices have the memory and processing capacity to support not only automatic speech recognition (ASR), but a whole range of multimedia functionalities that can be controlled with speech. Leveraging this newfound computational capacity is *Voice Command*, a C&C application for high-end mobile devices that allows users to look up contacts, place phone calls, retrieve appointments, obtain device status information, control multimedia and launch applications. It uses an embedded, speaker-independent recognizer and operates on 16 bit, 16 kHz, Mono audio.

Proceedings of SPEECHGRAM 2007, pages 33–40,
Prague, Czech Republic, June 2007.

OOG commands pose a serious threat to the usability of *Voice Command*. Many mobile users expect the product to "just work" without having to read the manual. So, if they should say *"Dial Bob"*, when the proper syntax for making a phone call is *Call {Name}*, the utterance will likely be misrecognized or dropped as a false recognition. If this happens enough, users may abandon the product, concluding that it or ASR in general, does not work.

2.1 OOG frequency

Given that C&C speech interaction is typically geared towards a relatively small number of words per utterance, an important question is, how often do OOG commands really occur in C&C? In *Project54* (Kun & Turner, 2005), a C&C application for retrieving police information in patrol cars, voice commands failed on average 15% of the time, roughly 63% of which were due to human error. Of that amount, roughly 54% were from extraneous words not found in the grammar, 12% from segmentation errors, and the rest from speaking commands that were not active.

To examine whether OOG commands might be as frequent on personal mobile devices, we collected over 9700 commands of roughly 1 to 3 seconds each from 204 real users of *Voice Command*, which were recorded as sound (.wav) files. We also logged all device data such as contact entries and media items. All sound files were transcribed by a paid professional transcription service. We ignored all transcriptions that did not have an associated command; the majority of such cases came from accidental pressing of the push-to-talk button. Furthermore, we focused on user-initiated commands, during which time the active grammar had the highest perplexity, instead of yes-no responses and clarification dialogue. This left 5061 transcribed utterances.

2.2 Emulation method

With the data transcribed, we first needed a method to distinguish between In-Grammar (ING) and OOG utterances. We developed a simulation environment built around a desktop version of the embedded recognizer which could load the same *Voice Command* grammars and update them with user device data, such as contact entries, for each sound file. It is important to note the desktop version was not the engine that is commercially shipped and optimized for particular devices, but rather one that serves testing and research purposes. The environment could not only recognize sound files, but also parse string input using the dynamically updated grammars as if that were the recognized result. We utilized the latter to emulate recognition of all transcribed utterances for *Voice Command*. If the parse succeeded, we labeled the utterance *ING*, otherwise it was labeled *OOG*.

Overall, we found that slightly more than one out of every four (1361 or 26.9%) transcribed utterances were OOG. We provide a complete breakdown of OOG types, including extraneous words and segmentation errors similar to Project54, in the next section. It is important to keep in mind that being OOG by emulation does not necessarily entail that the recognizer will fail on the actual sound file. For example, if a user states *"Call Bob at mobile phone"* when the word "phone" is OOG, the recognizer will still perform well. The OOG percentage for *Voice Command* may also reflect the high perplexity of the name-dialing task. Users had anywhere from 5 to over 2000 contacts, each of which could be expressed in multiple ways (e.g., first name, first name + last name, prefix + last name, etc.). In summary, our empirical analysis of the data suggests that OOG utterances for mobile C&C on personal devices can indeed occur on a frequent basis, and as such, are worth handling.

2.3 OOG type

In order to explore how we might handle different types of OOG commands, we classified them according to functional anatomy and basic edit operations. With respect to the former, a C&C utterance consists of three functional components:

1. **Slot**: A dynamically adjustable list representing a semantic argument, such as *{Contact}* or *{Date}*, where the value of the argument is typically one of the list members.
2. **Keyword**: A word or phrase that uniquely identifies a semantic predicate, such as *Call* or *Battery*, where the predicate corresponds in a one-to-one mapping to a type of command.
3. **Carrier Text**: A word or phrase that is designed to facilitate naturalistic expression of commands and carries no attached semantic content, such as "What is" or "Tell me".

OOGType	% Total	Description	Examples
Insertion	14.2%	adding a non-keyword, non-slot word	call britney porter on mobile phone ["phone" is superfluous]
Deletion	3.1%	deleting a non-keyword, non-slot word	my next appointments ["what are" missing]
Substitution	2.5%	replacing a non-keyword, non-slot word	where is my next appointment ["where" is not supported]
Segmentation	8.2%	incomplete utterance	show, call, start
Keyword Substitution	4.6%	replacing a keyword	call 8 8 2 8 0 8 0 ["dial" is keyword] , dial john horton ["call" is keyword]
Keyword Segmentation	0.1%	incomplete keyword	what are my appoint
Keyword Deletion	2.2%	deleting the keyword	marsha porter at home ["call" missing]
Slot Substitution	0.4%	replacing slot words	call executive 5 on desk ["desk" is not slot value]
Slot Segmentation	0.9%	incomplete slot	call alexander woods on mob
Slot Deletion	1.0%	deleted slot	call tracy morey at
Disfluencies	1.8%	disfluencies - mostly repetitions	start expense start microsoft excel
Order Rearrangement	0.6%	changing the order of words within a keyword	what meeting is next [Should be "what is my next meeting"]
Noise	0.7%	non primary speaker	oregon state home coming call brandon jones on mobile phone
OOG Slot	59.8%	The slot associated with this utterance is out of domain	Show Rich Lowry ["Richard" is contact entry] , dial 0 2 1 6 [Needs > 7 digits]

Table 1. Different OOG command types and their relative frequencies for the Voice Command product. The bracketed text in the "Examples" column explicates the cause of the error

For example, in the command *"Call Bob at mobile"*, the word "Call" is the keyword, "Bob" and "mobile" are slots, and "at" is a carrier word.

If we were to convert an ING command to match an OOG command, we could perform a series of edit operations: *substitution*, *deletion*, and *insertion*. For classifying OOG commands, substitution implies the use of an unexpected word, deletion implies the absence of an expected word, and insertion implies the addition of a superfluous word.

Starting with both functional anatomy and edit operations for classification, Table 1 displays the different types of OOG commands we labeled along with their relative frequencies. Because more than one label might apply to an utterance, we first looked to the slot for an OOG type label, then keyword, then everything else.

The most frequent OOG type, at about 60%, was *OOG Slot*, which referred to slot values that did not exist in the grammar. The majority of these cases came from two sources: 1) contact entries that users thought existed but did not – sometimes they did exist, but not in any normalized form (e.g., "Rich" for "Richard"), and 2) mislabeling of mostly foreign names by transcribers. Although we tried to correct as many names as we could, given the large contact lists that many users had, this proved to be quite challenging.

The second most frequent OOG type was *Insertion* at about 14%. The majority of these insertions were single words. Note that similar to Project54, segmentation errors occurred quite often at about 9%, when the different segmentation types are added together.

3 Backoff Approach

Having identified the different types of OOG commands, we needed to devise an approach for handling them that satisfied the requirements of *Voice Command* for supporting C&C on mobile devices.

3.1 Mobile requirements

For memory footprint, the *Voice Command* team specified that our approach should operate with less than 100KB of ROM and 1MB of RAM. Furthermore, the approach could not require changes

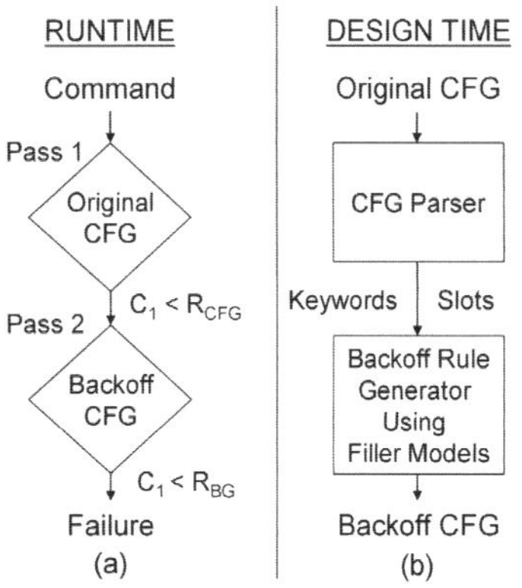

Figure 1. (a) A two-pass approach which leverages a base CFG for ING recognition and a backoff grammar for failed utterances. (b) Design time procedure for generating a backoff grammar

to the existing embedded Speech API (SAPI). Because the team also wanted to extend the functionality of *Voice Command* to new domains, we could not assume that we would have any data for training models. Although statistical language models (SLM) offer greater robustness to variations in phrasing than fixed grammars (Rosenfeld, 2000), the above requirements essentially prohibited them. So, we instead focused on extending the use of the base grammar, which for *Voice Command* was a context-free grammar (CFG): a formal specification of rules allowing for embedded recursion that defines the set of possible phrases (Manning & Schűtze, 1999).

Despite the manual effort that CFGs often require, they are widely prevalent in industry (Knight et al., 2001) for several reasons. First, they are easy for designers to understand and author. Second, they are easy to modify; new phrases can be added and immediately recognized with little effort. And third, they produce transparent semantics without requiring a separate natural language understanding component; semantic properties can be attached to CFG rules and assigned during recognition. By focusing on CFGs, our approach allows industry designers who are more accustomed to fixed grammars to continue using their skill set, while hopefully improving the handling of utterances that fall outside of their grammar.

3.2 Leveraging a backoff grammar

As long as utterances remain ING, a CFG affords fast and accurate recognition, especially because engines are often tuned to optimize C&C recognition. For example, in comparing recognition performance in a statistical and a CFG-based recognizer for the same domain, Knight et al. (2001) found that the CFG outperformed the SLM. In order to exploit the optimization of the engine for C&C utterances that are ING, we decided to utilize a two-pass approach where each command is initially submitted to the base CFG. If the confidence score of the top recognition C_1 falls below a rejection threshold R_{CFG}, or if the recognizer declares a false recognition (based on internal engine features), then the audio stream is passed to a backoff grammar which then attempts to recognize the command. If the backoff grammar fails to recognize the command, or the top recognition falls again below a rejection threshold R_{BG}, then users experience the same outcome as they normally would otherwise, except with a longer delay. Figure 1(a) summarizes the approach.

In order to generate the backoff grammar and still stay within the required memory bounds of *Voice Command*, we explored the use of the built-in filler or garbage model, which is a context-independent, acoustic phone loop. Expressed in the syntax as "...", filler models capture phones in whatever context they are placed. The functional anatomy of a C&C utterance, as explained in Section 2.3, sheds light on where to place them: before and/or after keywords and/or slots. As shown Figure 1(b), to construct a backoff grammar from a CFG during design time, we simply parse each CFG rule for keywords and slots, remove all carrier phrases, and insert filler models before and/or after the keywords and/or slots. Although it is straightforward to automatically identify keywords (words that uniquely map to a CFG rule) and slots (lists with semantic properties), developers may want to edit the generated backoff grammar for any keywords and slots they wish to exclude; for example, in cases where more than one keyword is found for a CFG rule.

For both slots and keywords, we could employ any number of different patterns for placing the filler models, if any. Table 2 displays some of the patterns in SAPI 5 format, which is an XML format where question marks indicate optional use. Although the Table is for keywords, the same patterns apply for slots. As shown in k_4, even the functional constituent itself can be optional. Furthermore, alternate lists of patterns can be composed, as in k_n. Depending on the number and type

Scheme	Keyword Pattern
k_1	<keyword/>
k_2	(…)? <keyword>
k_3	(…)? <keyword/> (…)?
k_4	(…)? <keyword/>? (…)?
k_n	<list> (…)? <keyword/>? (…)? (…) </list>

Table 2. Possible patterns in SAPI 5 XML format for placing the filler model, which appears as "...".Question marks indicate optional use.

of functional constituents for a CFG rule, backoff rules can be constructed by adjoining patterns for each constituent. We address the situation when a backoff rule corresponds to multiple CFG rules in Section 3.4.

3.3 Domain feasibility

Because every C&C utterance can be characterized by its functional constituents, the backoff filler approach generically applies to C&C domains, regardless of the actual keywords and slots. But the question remains, is this generic approach feasible for handling the different OOG types for *Voice Command* discussed in Section 2.3?

The filler model is clearly suited for *Insertions*, which are the second most frequent OOG type, because it would capture the additional phones. However, the most frequent OOG type, *OOG Slot*, cannot be handled by the backoff approach. That requires the developer to write better code for proper name normalization (e.g, "Rich" from "Richard") as well as breaking down the slot value into further components for better partial matching of names. Because new C&C domains may not utilize name slots, we decided to treat improving name recognition as separate research. Fortunately, opportunity for applying the backoff filler approach to *OOG Slot* types still exists.

3.4 Clarification of partial recognitions

As researchers have observed, OOG words contribute to increased word-error rates (Bazzi & Glass, 2000) and degrade the recognition performance of surrounding ING words (Gorrell, 2003). Hence, even if a keyword surrounding an OOG slot is recognized, its confidence score and the overall phrase confidence score will often be degraded. This is in some ways an unfortunate by-product of confidence annotation, which might be circumvented if SAPI exposed word lattice probabilities. Because SAPI does not, we can instead generate *partial backoff rules* that comprise only a subset of the functional constituents of a CFG rule. For example, if a CFG rule contains both a keyword and slot, then we can generate a partial backoff rule with just one or the other surrounded by filler models. Using partial backoff rules prevents degradation of confidence scores for ING constituents and improves partial recognitions, as we show in Section 4. Partial backoff rules not only handle *OOG Slot* commands where, for example, the name slot is not recognized, but also many types of segmentation, deletion and substitution commands as well.

Following prior research (Gorrell et al., 2002; Hockey et al., 2003), we sought to improve partial recognitions so that the system could provide feedback to users on what was recognized, and to encourage them to stay within the C&C syntax. Clarification dialogue with implicit instruction of the syntax might proceed as follows: If a partial recognition only corresponded to one CFG rule, then the system could assume the semantics of that rule and remind the user of the proper syntax. On the other hand, if a partial recognition corresponded to more than one rule, then a disambiguation dialogue could relate the proper syntax for the choices. For example, suppose a user says *"Telephone Bob"*, using the OOG word "Telephone". Although the original CFG would most likely misrecognize or even drop this command, our approach would obtain a partial recognition with higher confidence score for the contact slot. If only one CFG rule contained the slot, then the system could engage in the confirmation, *"Did you mean to say, call Bob?"* On the other hand, if more than one CFG rule contained the slot, then the system could engage in a disambiguation dialogue, such as *"I heard 'Bob'. You can either call or show Bob"*. Either way, the user is exposed to and implicitly taught the proper C&C syntax.

3.5 Related research

In related research, several researchers have investigated using both a CFG and a domain-trained SLM simultaneously for recognition (Gorrell et al., 2002; Hockey et al., 2003). To finesse the performance of a CFG, Gorrell (2003) advocated a two-pass approach where an SLM trained on CFG data (and slightly augmented) is utilized as a back-off grammar. However, only the performance of the SLM on a binary OOG classification task was evaluated and not the two-pass approach itself. In designing a multimodal language acquisition system, Dusan & Flanagan (2002) developed a two-pass approach where they utilized a dictation n-gram as a backoff grammar and added words recognized in the second pass into the base CFG. Unfortunately, they only evaluated the general usability of their architecture.

Because of the requirements outlined in Section 3.1, we have focused our efforts on generating a backoff grammar from the original CFG, taking advantage of functional anatomy and filler models. The approach is agnostic about what the actual filler model is, and as such, the built-in phone loop can easily be replaced by word-level (e.g., Yu et al., 2006) and sub-word level filler models (e.g., Liu et al., 2005). In fact, we did explore the word-level filler model, though so far we have not been able to meet the footprint requirements. We are currently investigating phone-based filler models.

Outside of recognition with a CFG, researchers have pursued methods that directly model OOG words as sub-word units in the recognition search space of a finite state transducer (FST) (Bazzi & Glass, 2000). OOG words can also be dynamically incorporated into the FST (Chung et al., 2004). Because this line of research depends on entirely different engine architecture, we could not apply the techniques.

4 Evaluation

In C&C speech interaction, what matters most is not word-error rate, but semantic accuracy and task completion. Because task completion is difficult to evaluate without collecting new data, we evaluated the semantic accuracy of the two-pass approach against the baseline of using just the CFG on the data we collected from real users, as discussed in Section 2.1. Furthermore, because partial recognitions can ultimately result in a successful dialogue, we carried out separate evaluations for the functional constituents of a command (i.e., keyword and slot) as well as the complete command (keyword + slot). For *Voice Command*, no command contained more than one slot, and because the vast majority of single slot commands were commands to either call or show a contact

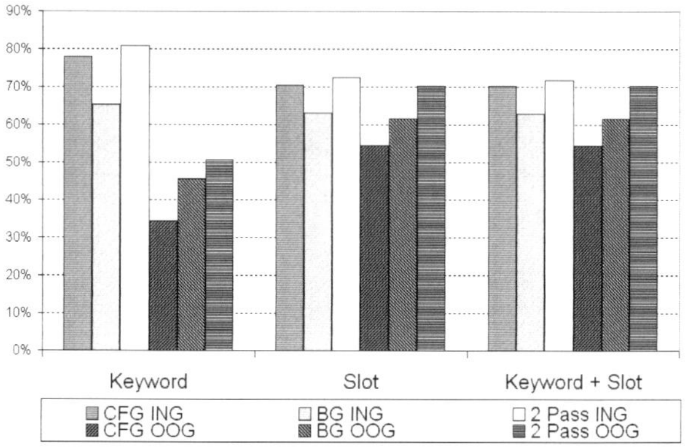

Figure 2. The semantic accuracies comparing the baseline CFG against both the BG (backoff grammar alone) and the two-pass approach (CFG + Backoff) separated into functional constituent groups and further separated by ING and OOG commands.

entry, we focused on those two commands as a proof of concept.

For any utterance, the recognizer can either accept or reject it. If it is accepted, then the semantics of the utterance can either be correct (i.e., it matches what the user intended) or incorrect. The following metrics can now be defined:

$$precision = CA / (CA + IA) \quad (1)$$

$$recall = CA / (CA + R) \quad (2)$$

$$accuracy = CA / (CA + IA + R) \quad (3)$$

where *CA* denotes accepted commands that are correct, *IA* denotes accepted commands that are incorrect, and *R* denotes the number of rejected commands. Although *R* could be decomposed into correct and incorrect rejections, for C&C, recognition failure is essentially perceived the same way by users: that is, as a non-understanding.

4.1 Results

For every C&C command in *Voice Command*, the embedded recognizer returns either a false recognition (based on internal engine parameters) or a recognition event with a confidence score. As described in Section 3.2, if the confidence score falls below a rejection threshold R_{CFG}, then the audio stream is processed by the backoff grammar which also enforces its own threshold R_{BG}. The R_{CFG} for *Voice Command* was set to 45% by a proprietary tuning procedure for optimizing acoustic word-error rate. For utterances that exceeded R_{CFG}, 84.2% of them were ING and 15.8% OOG. For utterances below R_{CFG}, 48.5%

		CFG	2-PASS	RER
Keyword	Prec	85.0%	79.0%	-39.7%
	Recall	36.8%	58.6%	34.5%
	Acc	**34.5%**	**50.7%**	**24.7%**
Slot	Prec	89.3%	88.2%	-10.3%
	Recall	58.1%	77.6%	46.5%
	Acc	**54.4%**	**70.3%**	**34.9%**
Keyword + Slot	Prec	89.3%	88.2%	-10.3%
	Recall	58.1%	77.6%	46.5%
	Acc	**54.4%**	**70.3%**	**34.9%**

Table 3. Relative reductions in semantic error rate, or Relative Error Reduction (RER) for OOG commands grouped by keyword, slot and keyword + slot evaluations. "2-PASS" denotes the two-pass approach.

were ING and 51.5% OOG. Because a considerable number of utterances may be ING in the second pass, as it was in our case, R_{BG} requires tuning as well. Instead of using a development dataset to tune R_{BG}, we decided to evaluate our approach on the entire data with R_{BG} set to the same proprietary threshold as R_{CFG}. In post-hoc analyses, this policy of setting the two thresholds equal and reverting to the CFG recognition if the backoff confidence score falls below R_{BG} achieved results comparable to optimizing the thresholds.

Figure 2 displays semantic accuracies separated by ING and OOG commands. Keyword evaluations comprised 3700 ING and 1361 OOG commands. Slot and keyword + slot evaluations comprised 2111 ING and 138 OOG commands. Overall, the two-pass approach was significantly higher in semantic accuracy than the baseline CFG, using McNemar's test ($p<0.001$). Not surprisingly, the largest gains were with OOG commands. Notice that for partial recognitions (i.e., keyword or slot only), the approach was able to improve accuracy, which with further clarification dialogue, could result in task completions. Interestingly, the approach performed the same for keyword + slot as it did for slot, which suggests that getting the slot correct is crucial to recognizing surrounding keywords. Despite the high percentage of OOG Slots, slot accuracy still increased due to better handling of other OOG types such as deletions, insertions and substitutions.

Finally, as a comparison, for the keyword + slot task, an upper bound of 74.3% ± 1.1% (10-fold cross-validated standard error) overall semantic accuracy was achieved using a small footprint statistical language modeling technique that re-ranked CFG results (Paek & Chickering, 2007), though the comparison is not completely fair given that the technique was focused on predictive language modeling and not on explicitly handling OOG utterances. Also note that in all cases, the backoff grammar alone performed worse than either the CFG or the two-pass approach.

Table 3 provides a more detailed view of the results for the just OOG commands as well as the relative reductions in semantic error rate (RER). Notice that the approach increases recall, which signifies less non-understandings. However, this comes at the price of a small increase in misunderstandings, as seen in the decrease in precision. Overall, the best reduction in semantic error rate achieved by the approach was about 35%.

Decomposing RER by OOG types, we found that for keyword evaluations, the biggest improvement (52% RER), came about for *Deletion* types, or commands with missing carrier words. This makes sense because the backoff grammar only cares about the keyword. For slot and keyword + slot evaluations, *Insertion* types maintained the biggest improvement at 38% RER.

Note that the results presented are those obtained without tuning. If application developers wanted to find an optimal operating point, they would need to decide what is more important for their application: precision or recall, and adjust the thresholds until they reach acceptable levels of performance. Ideally, these levels should accord with what real users of the application would accept.

4.2 Efficiency

Given that the approach was aimed at satisfying the mobile requirements stated in Section 3.1, which it did, we also compared the processing time it takes to arrive at a recognition or false recognition between the CFG alone and the two-pass approach. Because of the filler models, the backoff grammar is a more relaxed version of CFG with a larger search space, and as such, takes slightly more processing time. The average processing time for the CFG in our simulation environment was about 395 milliseconds, whereas the average processing time for the two passes was about 986 milliseconds. Hence, when the backoff grammar is used, the total computation time is approximately 2.5 times that of a single pass alone. In our experiments, a total of 1570 commands (i.e. 31%) required the two passes, while 3491 of them were accepted after a single CFG pass.

4.3 Drawbacks

In exploring the backoff filler approach, we encountered a few drawbacks that are worth considering when applying this approach to other domains. The first issue dealt with false positives. In the data collection for *Voice Command*, a total of 288 utterances contained no discernable speech. If these were included in the data set, they would amount to about 5% of all utterances. As mentioned previously, these were mostly cases when the push-to-talk button was accidentally triggered. When we evaluated the approach on these utterances, we found that the CFG accepted 36 or roughly 13% of them, while the proposed approach accepted 115 or roughly 40% of them. For our domain, this problem can be avoided by instructing users to lock their devices when not in use to prevent spurious initiations. For other C&C domains where unintentional command initiations occur frequently, this may be a serious concern, though we suspect that users will be more forgiving of accidental errors than real errors.

Another drawback dealt with generating the backoff grammar. As we discussed in Section 3.2, various patterns for placing filler models can be utilized. Although we did explore the possibility that perhaps certain patterns might generalize across domains, we found that it was better to hand-craft patterns to the application. For *Voice Command*, we used the k_n pattern specified in Table 2 for keywords, and the identical s_n pattern for slots because they proved to be best suited to the product grammars in pre-trial experiments.

5 Conclusion & Future Direction

In this paper, we classified the different types of OOG commands that might occur in a mobile C&C application, and presented a simple two-pass approach for handling them that leverages the base CFG for ING recognition and a backoff grammar OOG recognition. The backoff grammar is generated from the original CFG by surrounding keywords and/or slots with filler models. Operating within the memory footprint requirements of a mobile C&C product, the approach yielded a 35% relative reduction in semantic error rate for OOG commands, and improved partial recognitions, which can facilitate clarification dialogue.

We are now exploring small footprint, phone-based filler models. Another avenue for future research is to further investigate optimal policies for deciding when to pass to the backoff grammar and when to use the backoff grammar recognition.

References

I. Bazzi & J. Glass. 2000. *Modeling out-of-vocabulary words for robust speech recognition.* In Proc. ICSLP.

G. Chung, S. Seneff, C.Wang, & I. Hetherington. 2004. *A dynamic vocabulary spoken dialogue interface.* In Proc. ICSLP.

S. Dusan & J. Flanagan. 2002. *Adaptive dialog based upon multimodal language acquisition.* In Proc. ICMI.

G. Gorrell, I. Lewin, & M. Rayner. 2002. *Adding intelligent help to mixed initiative spoken dialogue systems.* In Proc. ICSLP.

G. Gorrell. 2003. *Using statistical language modeling to identify new vocabulary in a grammar-based speech recognition system.* In Proc. Eurospeech.

B. Hockey, O. Lemon, E. Campana, L. Hiatt, G. Aist, J. Hieronymus, A. Gruenstein, & J. Dowding. 2003. *Targeted help for spoken dialogue systems: intelligent feedback improves naive users' performance.* In Proc. EACL, pp. 147–154.

S. Knight, G. Gorrell, M. Rayner, D. Milward, R. Koeling, & I. Lewin. 2001. *Comparing grammar-based and robust approaches to speech understanding: A case study.* In Proc. Eurospeech.

A. Kun & L. Turner. 2005. *Evaluating the project54 speech user interface.* In Proc. Pervasive.

P. Liu, Y. Tian, J. Zhou, & F. Soong. 2005. *Background model based posterior probability for measuring confidence.* In Proc. Interspeech.

C.D. Manning & H. Sch¨utze. 1999. *Foundations of Statistical Natural Language Processing.* MIT Press, Cambridge,Massachusetts.

Paek, T. & Chickering, D. 2007. *Improving command and control speech recognition: Using predictive user models for language modeling.* UMUAI, 17(1):93-117.

Rosenfeld, R. 2000. Two decades of statistical language modeling: Where do we go from here? In Proc. of the IEEE, 88(8): 1270–1278.

R. Rosenfeld, D. Olsen, & A. Rudnicky. 2001. *Universal speech interfaces.* Interactions, 8(6):34–44.

D. Yu, Y.C. Ju, Y. Wang, & A. Acero. 2006. *N-gram based filler model for robust grammar authoring.* In Proc. ICASSP.

A Bidirectional Grammar-Based Medical Speech Translator

Pierrette Bouillon[1], **Glenn Flores**[2], **Marianne Starlander**[1], **Nikos Chatzichrisafis**[1]
Marianne Santaholma[1], **Nikos Tsourakis**[1], **Manny Rayner**[1,3], **Beth Ann Hockey**[4]

[1] University of Geneva, TIM/ISSCO, 40 bvd du Pont-d'Arve, CH-1211 Geneva 4, Switzerland
Pierrette.Bouillon@issco.unige.ch
Marianne.Starlander@eti.unige.ch, Nikos.Chatzichrisafis@vozZup.com
Marianne.Santaholma@eti.unige.ch, Nikolaos.Tsourakis@issco.unige.ch

[2] Medical College of Wisconsin, 8701 Watertown Plank Road, Milwaukee, WI 53226
gflores@mcw.edu

[3] Powerset, Inc., 475 Brannan Street, San Francisco, CA 94107
manny@powerset.com

[4] Mail Stop 19-26, UCSC UARC, NASA Ames Research Center, Moffett Field, CA 94035–1000
bahockey@ucsc.edu

Abstract

We describe a bidirectional version of the grammar-based MedSLT medical speech system. The system supports simple medical examination dialogues about throat pain between an English-speaking physician and a Spanish-speaking patient. The physician's side of the dialogue is assumed to consist mostly of WH-questions, and the patient's of elliptical answers. The paper focusses on the grammar-based speech processing architecture, the ellipsis resolution mechanism, and the online help system.

1 Background

There is an urgent need for medical speech translation systems. The world's current population of 6.6 billion speaks more than 6,000 languages (Graddol, 2004). Language barriers are associated with a wide variety of deleterious consequences in healthcare, including impaired health status, a lower likelihood of having a regular physician, lower rates of mammograms, pap smears, and other preventive services, non-adherence with medications, a greater likelihood of a diagnosis of more severe psychopathology and leaving the hospital against medical advice among psychiatric patients, a lower likelihood of being given a follow-up appointment after an emergency department visit, an increased risk of intubation among children with asthma, a greater risk of hospital admissions among adults, an increased risk of drug complications, longer medical visits, higher resource utilization for diagnostic testing, lower patient satisfaction, impaired patient understanding of diagnoses, medications, and follow-up, and medical errors and injuries (Flores, 2005; Flores, 2006). Nevertheless, many patients who need medical interpreters do not get them. For example, in the United States, where 52 million people speak a language other than English at home and 23 million people have limited English proficiency (LEP) (Census, 2007), one study found that about half of LEP patients presenting to an emergency department were not provided with a medical interpreter (Baker et al., 1996). There is thus a substantial gap between the need for and availability of language services in health care, a gap that could be bridged through effective medical speech translation systems.

An ideal system would be able to interpret accurately and flexibly between patients and health care professionals, using unrestricted language and a large vocabulary. A system of this kind is, unfortunately, beyond the current state of the art. It is, however, possible, using today's technology, to build speech translation systems for specific scenarios and language-pairs, which can achieve acceptable levels of reliability within the bounds

Proceedings of SPEECHGRAM 2007, pages 41–48,
Prague, Czech Republic, June 2007.

of a well-defined controlled language. MedSLT (Bouillon et al., 2005) is an Open Source system of this type, which has been under construction at Geneva University since 2003. The system is built on top of Regulus (Rayner et al., 2006), an Open Source platform which supports development of grammar-based speech-enabled applications. Regulus has also been used to build several other systems, including NASA's Clarissa (Rayner et al., 2005b).

The most common architecture for speech translation today uses statistical methods to perform both speech recognition and translation, so it is worth clarifying why we have chosen to use grammar-based methods. Even though statistical architectures exhibit many desirable properties (purely data-driven, domain independent), this is not necessarily the best alternative in safety-critical medical applications. Anecdotally, many physicians express reluctance to trust a translation device whose output is not readily predictable, and most of the speech translation systems which have reached the stage of field testing rely on various types of grammar-based recognition and rule-based translation (Phraselator, 2007; Fluential, 2007).

Statistical speech recognisers can achieve impressive levels of accuracy when trained on enough data, but it is a daunting task to collect training material in the requisite quantities (usually, tens of thousands of high-quality utterances) when trying to build practical systems. Considering that the medical speech translation applications we are interested in constructing here need to work for multiple languages and subdomains, the problem becomes even more challenging. Our experience is that grammar-based systems which also incorporate probabilistic context-free grammar tuning deliver better results than purely statistical ones when training data are sparse (Rayner et al., 2005a).

Another common criticism of grammar-based systems is that out-of-coverage utterances will neither be recognized nor translated, an objection that critics have sometimes painted as decisive. It is by no means obvious, however, that restricted coverage is such a serious problem. In text processing, work on several generations of controlled language systems has developed a range of techniques for keeping users within the bounds of system coverage (Kittredge, 2003; Mitamura, 1999), and variants of these methods can also be adapted for spoken language applications. Our experiments with MedSLT show that even a quite simple help system is enough to guide users quickly towards the intended coverage of a medium-vocabulary grammar-based speech translation application, with most users appearing confident after just an hour or two of exposure (Starlander et al., 2005; Chatzichrisafis et al., 2006).

Until recently, the MedSLT system only supported unidirectional processing in the physician to patient direction. The assumption was that the physician would mostly ask yes/no questions, to which the patient would respond non-verbally, for example by nodding or shaking their head. A unidirectional architecture is easier to make habitable than a bidirectional one. It is reasonable to assume that the physician will use the system regularly enough to learn the coverage, but most patients will not have used the system before, and it is less clear that they will be able to acclimatize within the narrow window at their disposal. These considerations must however be balanced against the fact that a unidirectional system does not allow for a patient-centered interaction characterized by meaningful patient-clinician communication or shared decision making. Multiple studies in the medical literature document that patient-centeredness, effective patient-clinician communication, and shared decision making are associated with significant improvements in patient health outcomes, including reduced anxiety levels, improved functional status, reduced pain, better control of diabetes mellitus, blood pressure reduction among hypertensives, improved adherence, increased patient satisfaction, and symptom reduction for a variety of conditions (Stewart, 1995; Michie et al., 2003). A bidirectional system is considered close to essential from a healthcare perspective, since it appropriately addresses the key issues of patient centeredness and shared decision making. For these reasons, we have over the last few months developed a bidirectional version of MedSLT, initially focussing on a throat pain scenario with an English-speaking physician and a Spanish-speaking patient. The physician uses full sentences, while the patient answers with short responses.

One of the strengths of the Regulus approach is

that it is very easy to construct parallel versions of a grammar; generally, all that is required is to vary the training corpus. (We will have more to say about this soon). We have exploited these properties of the platform to create two different configurations of the bidirectional system, so that we can compare competing approaches to the problem of accommodating patients unfamiliar with speech technology. In Version 1 (less restricted), the patient is allowed to answer using both elliptical utterances and short sentences, while in Version 2 (more restricted) they are only permitted to use elliptical utterances. Thus, for example, if the physician asks the question "How long have you had a sore throat?", Version 1 allows the patient to respond both "Desde algunos días" ("For several days") and "Me ha dolido la garganta desde algunos días" ("I have had a sore throat for several days"), while Version 2 only allows the first of these. Both the short and the long versions are translated uniformly, with the short version resolved using the context from the preceding question.

In both versions, if the patient finds it too challenging to use the system to answer WH-questions directly, it is possible to back off to the earlier dialogue architecture in which the physician uses Y-N questions and the patient responds with simple yes/no answers, or nonverbally. Continuing the example, if the patient is unable to find an appropriate way to answer the physician's question, the physician could ask "Have you had a sore throat for more than three days?"; if the patient responds negatively, they could continue with the follow-on question "More than a week?", and so on.

In the rest of the paper, we first describe the system top-level (Section 2), the way in which grammar-based processing is used (Section 3), the ellipsis processing mechanism (Section 4), and the help system (Section 5). Section 6 presents an initial evaluation, and the final section concludes.

2 Top-level architecture

The system is operated through the graphical user interface (GUI) shown in Figures 1 and 2. In accordance with the basic principles of patient-centeredness and shared decision-making outlined in Section 1, the patient and the physician each have their own headset, use their own mouse, and share the same view of the screen. This is in sharp contrast to the majority of the medical speech translation systems described in the literature (Somers, 2006).

As shown in the screenshots, the main GUI window is separated into two tabbed panes, marked "Doctor" and "Patient". Initially, the "Doctor" view (the one shown in Figure 1) is active. The physician presses the "Push to talk" button, and speaks into the headset microphone. If recognition is successful, the GUI displays four separate results, listed on the right side of the screen. At the top, immediately under the heading "Question", we can see the actual words returned by speech recognition. Here, these words are "Have you had rapid strep test". Below, we have the help pane: this displays similar questions taken from the help corpus, which are known to be within system coverage. The pane marked "System understood" shows a back-translation, produced by first translating the recognition result into interlingua, and then translating it back into English. In the present example, this corrects the minor mistake the recogniser has made, missing the indefinite article "a", and confirms that the system has obtained a correct grammatical analysis and interpretation at the level of interlingua. At the bottom, we see the target language translation. The left-hand side of the screen logs the history of the conversation to date, so that both sides can refer back to it.

If the physician decides that the system has correctly understood what they said, they can now press the "Play" button. This results in the system producing a spoken output, using the Vocalizer TTS engine. Simultaneously with speaking, the GUI shifts to the "Patient" configuration shown in Figure 2. This differs from the "Doctor" configuration in two respects: all text is in the patient language, and the help pane presents its suggestions immediately, based on the preceding physician question. The various processing components used to support these functionalities are described in the following sections.

3 Grammar-based processing

Grammar-based processing is used for source-language speech recognition and target-side generation. (Source-language analysis is part of the recognition process, since grammar-based recognition includes creating a parse). All of these functionalities

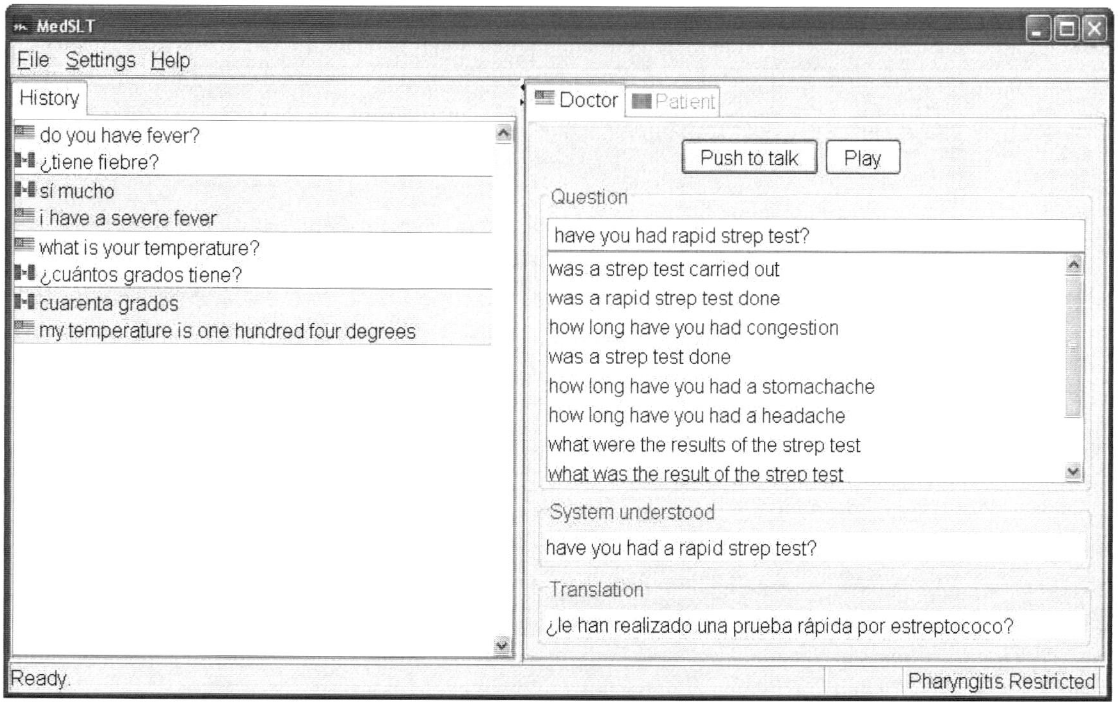

Figure 1: Screenshot showing the state of the GUI after the physician has spoken, but before he has pressed the "Play" button. The help pane shows similar queries known to be within coverage.

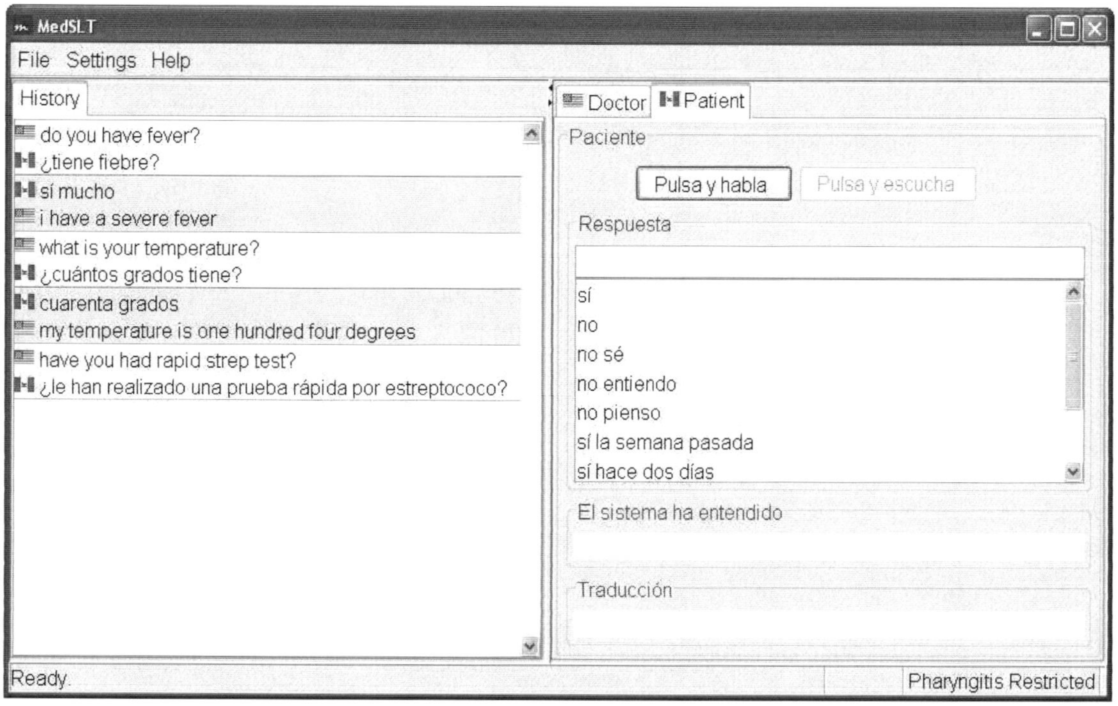

Figure 2: Screenshot showing the state of the GUI after the physician has pressed the "Play" button. The help pane shows known valid responses to similar questions.

are implemented using the Regulus platform, with the task-specific grammars compiled out of general feature grammar resources by the Regulus tools. For both recognition and generation, the first step is to extract a domain-specific feature grammar from the general one, using a version of the Explanation Based Learning (EBL) algorithm.

The extraction process is driven by a corpus of examples and a set of "operationality criteria", which define how the rules in the original resource grammar are recombined into domain-specific ones. It is important to realise that the domain-specific grammar is *not* merely a subset of the resource grammar; a typical domain-specific grammar rule is created by merging two to five resource grammar rules into a single "flatter" rule. The result is a feature grammar which is less general than the original one, but more efficient. For recognition, the grammar is then processed further into a CFG language model, using an algorithm which alternates expansion of feature values and filtering of the partially expanded grammar to remove irrelevant rules. Detailed descriptions of the EBL learning and feature grammar → CFG compilation algorithms can be found in Chapters 8 and 10 of (Rayner et al., 2006). Regulus feature grammars can also be compiled into generators using a version of the Semantic Head Driven algorithm (Shieber et al., 1990).

The English (physician) side recogniser is compiled from the large English resource grammar described in Chapter 9 of (Rayner et al., 2006), and was constructed in the same way as the one described in (Rayner et al., 2005a), which was used for a headache examination task. The operationality criteria are the same, and the only changes are a different training corpus and the addition of new entries to the lexicon. The same resources, with a different training corpus, were used to build the English language generator. It is worth pointing out that, although a uniform method was used to build these various grammars, the results were all very different. For example, the recognition grammar from (Rayner et al., 2005a) is specialised to cover only second-person questions ("Do you get headaches in the mornings?"), while the generator grammar used in the present application covers only first-person declarative statements ("I visited the doctor last Monday."). In terms of structure, each grammar contains several important constructions that the other lacks. For example, subordinate clauses are central in the headache domain ("Do the headaches occur when you are stressed?") but are not present in the sore throat domain; this is because the standard headache examination questions mostly focus on generic conditions, while the sore throat examination questions only relate to concrete ones. Conversely, relative clauses are important in the sore throat domain ("I have recently been in contact with someone who has strep throat"), but are not sufficiently important in the headache domain to be covered there.

On the Spanish (patient) side, there are four grammars involved. For recognition, we have two different grammars, corresponding to the two versions of the system; the grammar for Version 2 is essentially a subset of that for Version 1. For generation, there are two separate and quite different grammars: one is used for translating the physician's questions, while the other produces back-translations of the patient's questions. All of these grammars are extracted from a general shared resource grammar for Romance languages, which currently combines rules for French, Spanish and Catalan (Bouillon et al., 2006; Bouillon et al., to appear 2007b).

One interesting consequence of our methodology is related to the fact that Spanish is a prodrop language, which implies that many sentences are systematically ambiguous between declarative and Y-N question readings. For example, "He consultado un médico" could in principle mean either "I visited a doctor" or "Did I visit a doctor?". When training the specialised Spanish grammars, it is thus necessary to specify which readings of the training sentences are to be used. Continuing the example, if the sentence occurred in training material for the answer grammar, we would specify that the declarative reading was the intended one[1].

4 Ellipsis processing and contextual interpretation

In Version 1 of the system, the patient is permitted to answer using elliptical phrases; in Ver-

[1]The specification can be formulated as a preference that applies uniformly to all the training examples in a given group.

sion 2, she is obliged to do so. Ability to process elliptical responses makes it easier to guide the patient towards the intended coverage of the system, without degrading the quality of recognition (Bouillon et al., to appear 2007a). The downside is that ellipses are also harder to translate than full sentences. Even in a limited domain like ours, and in a closely related language-pair, ellipsis can generally not be translated word for word, and it is necessary to look at the preceding context if the rules are to be applied correctly. In examples 1 and 2 below, the locative phrase "In your stomach" in the English source becomes the subject in the Spanish translation. This implies that the translation of the ellipsis in the second physician utterance needs to change syntactic category: "In your head" (PP) becomes "La cabeza" (NP).

(1)	Doctor:	Do you have a pain in your stomach?
	(Trans):	Le duele el estomago?
(2)	Doctor:	In your head?
	(Trans):	*En la cabeza?

Since examples like this are frequent, our system implements a solution in which the patient's replies are translated in the context of the preceding utterance. If the patient-side recogniser's output is classified as an ellipsis (this can done fairly reliably thanks to use of suitably specialised grammars; cf. Section 3), we expand the incomplete phrase into a full sentence structure by adding appropriate structural elements from the preceding physician-side question; the expanded semantic structure is the one which is then translated into interlingual form, and thence back to the physician-side language.

Since all linguistic representations, including those of elliptical phrases and their contexts, are represented as flat attribute-value lists, we are able to implement the resolution algorithm very simply in terms of list manipulation. In YN-questions, where the elliptical answer intuitively adds information to the question ("Did you visit the doctor?"; "El lunes" → "I visited the doctor on Monday"), the representations are organised so that resolution mainly amounts to concatenation of the two lists[2]. In WH-questions, where the answer intuitively substitutes the elliptical answer for the WH-phrase ("What is your temperature?"; "Cuarenta grados" → "My temperature is forty degrees"), resolution substitutes the representation of the elliptical phrase for that of a semantically similar element in the question.

The least trivial aspect of this process is providing a suitable definition of "semantically similar". This is done using a simple example-based method, in which the grammar developer writes a set of declarations, each of which lists a set of semantically similar NPs. At compile-time, the grammar is used to parse each NP, and extract a generalised skeleton, in which specific lexical information is stripped away; at run-time, two NPs are held to be semantically similar if they can each be unified with skeletons in the same equivalence class. This ensures that the definition of the semantic similarity relation is stable across most changes to the grammar and lexicon. The issues are described in greater detail in (Bouillon et al., to appear 2007a).

5 Help system

Since the performance of grammar-based speech understanding is only reliable on in-coverage material, systems based on this type of architecture must necessarily use a controlled language approach, in which it is assumed that the user is able to learn the relevant coverage. As previously noted, the MedSLT system addresses this problem by incorporating an online help system (Starlander et al., 2005; Chatzichrisafis et al., 2006).

On the physician side, the help system offers, after each recognition event, a list of related questions; similarly, on the patient side, it provides examples of known valid answers to the current question. In both cases, the help examples are extracted from a precompiled corpus of question-answer pairs, which have been judged for correctness by system developers. The process of selecting the examples is slightly different on the two sides. For questions (physician side), the system performs a second parallel recognition of the input speech, using a statistical recogniser. It then compares the recognition result, using an N-gram based metric, against the set of known correct in-coverage questions from the question-answer corpus, to extract the most similar ones. For answers (patient side), the help system searches the question-answer corpus to find the

[2] It is also necessary to replace second-person pronouns with first-person counterparts.

questions most similar to the current one, and shows the list of corresponding valid answers, using the whole list in the case of Version 1 of the system, and only the subset consisting of elliptical phrases in the case of Version 2.

6 Evaluation

In previous studies, we have evaluated speech recognition and speech understanding performance for physician-side questions in English (Bouillon et al., 2005) and Spanish (Bouillon et al., to appear 2007b), and investigated the impact on performance of the help system (Rayner et al., 2005a; Starlander et al., 2005). We have also carried out recent evaluations designed to contrast recognition performance on elliptical and full versions of the same utterance; here, our results suggest that elliptical forms of (French-language) MedSLT utterances are slightly easier to recognise in terms of semantic error rate than full sentential forms (Bouillon et al., to appear 2007a). Our initial evaluation studies on the bidirectional system have focussed on a specific question which has particular relevance to this new version of MedSLT. Since we are assuming that the patient will respond using elliptical utterances, and that these utterances will be translated in the context of the preceding physician-side question, how confident can we be that this context-dependent translation will be correct?

In order to investigate these issues, we performed a small data-collection using Version 2 of the system, whose results we summarise here. One of the authors of the paper played the role of an English-speaking physician, in a simulated medical examination scenario where the goal was to determine whether or not the "patient" was suffering from a viral throat infection. The six subjects playing the role of the patient were all native speakers of Spanish, and had had no previous exposure to the system, or indeed any kind of speech technology. They were given cards describing the symptoms they were supposed to be displaying, on which they were asked to based their answers. From a total of 92 correctly recognised patient responses, we obtained 50 yes/no answers and 42 examples of real elliptical utterances. Out of these, 36 were judged to have been translated completely correctly, and a further 3 were judged correct in terms of meaning, but less than fluent. Only 3 examples were badly translated: of these two were caused by problems in a translation rule, and one by incorrect treatment of ellipsis resolution. We show representative exchanges below; the last of these is the one in which ellipsis processing failed to work correctly.

(3)	Doctor:	For how long have you had your sore throat?
	Patient:	Desde hace más de una semana
	(Trans):	I have had a sore throat for more than one week
(4)	Doctor:	What were the results?
	Patient:	Negativo
	(Trans):	The results were negative
(5)	Doctor:	Have you seen a doctor for your sore throat?
	Patient:	Sí el lunes
	(Trans):	I visited the doctor for my sore throat monday
(6)	Doctor:	Have you been with anyone recently who has a strep throat?
	Patient:	Si más de dos semanas
	(Trans):	I was in contact with someone more than two weeks recently who had strep throat

7 Conclusions

We have presented a bidirectional grammar-based English ↔ Spanish medical speech translation system built using a linguistically motivated architecture, where all linguistic information is ultimately derived from two resource grammars, one for each language. We have shown how this enables us to derive the multiple grammars needed, which differ both with respect to function (recognition/generation) and to domain (physician questions/patient answers). The system is currently undergoing initial lab testing; we hope to advance to initial trials on real patients some time towards the end of the year.

References

[Baker et al.1996] D.W. Baker, R.M. Parker, M.V. Williams, W.C. Coates, and Kathryn Pitkin. 1996.

Use and effectiveness of interpreters in an emergency department. *Journal of the American Medical Association*, 275:783–8.

[Bouillon et al.2005] P. Bouillon, M. Rayner, N. Chatzichrisafis, B.A. Hockey, M. Santaholma, M. Starlander, Y. Nakao, K. Kanzaki, and H. Isahara. 2005. A generic multi-lingual open source platform for limited-domain medical speech translation. In *Proceedings of the 10th Conference of the European Association for Machine Translation (EAMT)*, pages 50–58, Budapest, Hungary.

[Bouillon et al.2006] P. Bouillon, M. Rayner, B. Novellas Vall, Y. Nakao, M. Santaholma, M. Starlander, and N. Chatzichrisafis. 2006. Une grammaire multilingue partagée pour la traduction automatique de la parole. In *Proceedings of TALN 2006*, Leuwen, Belgium.

[Bouillon et al.to appear 2007a] P. Bouillon, M. Rayner, M. Santaholma, and M. Starlander. to appear 2007a. Les ellipses dans un système de traduction automatique de la parole. In *Proceedings of TALN 2006*, Toulouse, France.

[Bouillon et al.to appear 2007b] P. Bouillon, M. Rayner, B. Novellas Vall, Y. Nakao, M. Santaholma, M. Starlander, and N. Chatzichrisafis. to appear 2007b. Une grammaire partagée multi-tâche pour le traitement de la parole : application aux langues romanes. *Traitement Automatique des Langues*.

[Census2007] U.S. Census, 2007. *Selected Social Characteristics in the United States: 2005. Data Set: 2005 American Community Survey*. Available here.

[Chatzichrisafis et al.2006] N. Chatzichrisafis, P. Bouillon, M. Rayner, M. Santaholma, M. Starlander, and B.A. Hockey. 2006. Evaluating task performance for a unidirectional controlled language medical speech translation system. In *Proceedings of the HLT-NAACL International Workshop on Medical Speech Translation*, pages 9–16, New York.

[Flores2005] G. Flores. 2005. The impact of medical interpreter services on the quality of health care: A systematic review. *Medical Care Research and Review*, 62:255–299.

[Flores2006] G. Flores. 2006. Language barriers to health care in the united states. *New England Journal of Medicine*, 355:229–231.

[Fluential2007] Fluential, 2007. http://www.fluentialinc.com. As of 24 March 2007.

[Graddol2004] D. Graddol. 2004. The future of language. *Science*, 303:1329–1331.

[Kittredge2003] R. I. Kittredge. 2003. Sublanguages and comtrolled languages. In R. Mitkov, editor, *The Oxford Handbook of Computational Linguistics*, pages 430–447. Oxford University Press.

[Michie et al.2003] S. Michie, J. Miles, and J. Weinman. 2003. Patient-centeredness in chronic illness: what is it and does it matter? *Patient Education and Counseling*, 51:197–206.

[Mitamura1999] T. Mitamura. 1999. Controlled language for multilingual machine translation. In *Proceedings of Machine Translation Summit VII*, Singapore.

[Phraselator2007] Phraselator, 2007. http://www.voxtec.com/. As of 24 March 2007.

[Rayner et al.2005a] M. Rayner, P. Bouillon, N. Chatzichrisafis, B.A. Hockey, M. Santaholma, M. Starlander, H. Isahara, K. Kanzaki, and Y. Nakao. 2005a. A methodology for comparing grammar-based and robust approaches to speech understanding. In *Proceedings of the 9th International Conference on Spoken Language Processing (ICSLP)*, pages 1103–1107, Lisboa, Portugal.

[Rayner et al.2005b] M. Rayner, B.A. Hockey, J.M. Renders, N. Chatzichrisafis, and K. Farrell. 2005b. A voice enabled procedure browser for the International Space Station. In *Proceedings of the 43rd Annual Meeting of the Association for Computational Linguistics (interactive poster and demo track)*, Ann Arbor, MI.

[Rayner et al.2006] M. Rayner, B.A. Hockey, and P. Bouillon. 2006. *Putting Linguistics into Speech Recognition: The Regulus Grammar Compiler*. CSLI Press, Chicago.

[Shieber et al.1990] S. Shieber, G. van Noord, F.C.N. Pereira, and R.C. Moore. 1990. Semantic-head-driven generation. *Computational Linguistics*, 16(1).

[Somers2006] H. Somers. 2006. Language engineering and the path to healthcare: a user-oriented view. In *Proceedings of the HLT-NAACL International Workshop on Medical Speech Translation*, pages 32–39, New York.

[Starlander et al.2005] M. Starlander, P. Bouillon, N. Chatzichrisafis, M. Santaholma, M. Rayner, B.A. Hockey, H. Isahara, K. Kanzaki, and Y. Nakao. 2005. Practising controlled language through a help system integrated into the medical speech translation system (MedSLT). In *Proceedings of MT Summit X*, Phuket, Thailand.

[Stewart1995] M.A. Stewart. 1995. Effective physician-patient communication and health outcomes: a review. *Canadian Medical Association Journal*, 152:1423–1433.

A Development Environment for Building Grammar-Based Speech-Enabled Applications

Elisabeth Kron[1], **Manny Rayner**[1,2], **Marianne Santaholma**[1], **Pierrette Bouillon**[1]

[1] **University of Geneva, TIM/ISSCO**
40 bvd du Pont-d'Arve
CH-1211 Geneva 4, Switzerland
elisabethkron@yahoo.co.uk
Marianne.Santaholma@eti.unige.ch
Pierrette.Bouillon@issco.unige.ch

[2] **Powerset, Inc.**
475 Brannan Street
San Francisco, CA 94107
manny@powerset.com

Abstract

We present a development environment for Regulus, a toolkit for building unification grammar-based speech-enabled systems, focussing on new functionality added over the last year. In particular, we will show an initial version of a GUI-based top-level for the development environment, a tool that supports graphical debugging of unification grammars by cutting and pasting of derivation trees, and various functionalities that support systematic development of speech translation and spoken dialogue applications built using Regulus.

1 The Regulus platform

The Regulus platform is a comprehensive toolkit for developing grammar-based speech-enabled systems that can be run on the commercially available Nuance recognition environment. The platform has been developed by an Open Source consortium, the main partners of which have been NASA Ames Research Center and Geneva University, and is freely available for download from the SourceForge website[1]. Regulus has been used to build several large systems, including Geneva University's MedSLT medical speech translator (Bouillon et al., 2005) and NASA's Clarissa procedure browser (Rayner et al., 2005b)[2].

Regulus is described at length in (Rayner et al., 2006), the first half of which consists of an extended tutorial introduction. The release also includes extensive online documentation, including several example applications.

The core functionality offered by Regulus is compilation of typed unification grammars into parsers, generators, and Nuance-formatted CFG language models, and hence also into Nuance recognition packages. Small unification grammars can be compiled directly into executable forms. The central idea of Regulus, however, is to base as much of the development work as possible on large, domain-independent resource grammars. A resource grammar for English is available from the Regulus website; similar grammars for several other languages have been developed under the MedSLT project at Geneva University, and can be downloaded from the MedSLT SourceForge website[3].

Large resource grammars of this kind are over-general as they stand, and it is not possible to compile them directly into efficient recognisers or generators. The platform, however, provides tools, driven by small corpora of examples, that can be used to create specialised versions of these general grammars using the Explanation Based Learning (EBL) algorithm. We have shown in a series of experiments that suitably specialised grammars can be compiled into efficient executable forms. In particular, recognisers built in this way are very competitive with ones created using statistical training methods (Rayner et al., 2005a).

The Regulus platform also supplies a framework for using the compiled resources — parsers, generators and recognisers — to build speech translation and spoken dialogue applications. The environment currently supports 75 different commands,

[1] http://sourceforge.net/projects/regulus/
[2] http://ic.arc.nasa.gov/projects/clarissa/
[3] http://sourceforge.net/projects/medslt

Proceedings of SPEECHGRAM 2007, pages 49–52,
Prague, Czech Republic, June 2007.

which can be used to carry out a range of functions including compilation of grammars into various forms, debugging of grammars and compiled resources, and testing of applications. The environment exists in two forms. The simpler one, which has been available from the start of the project, is a command-line interface embedded within the SICStus Prolog top-level. The focus will however be on a new GUI-based environment, which has been under development since late 2006, and which offers a more user-friendly graphical/menu-based view of the underlying functionality.

In the rest of the paper, we outline how Regulus supports development both at the level of grammars (Section 2), and at the level of the applications that can be built using the executable forms derived from them (Section 3).

2 Developing unification grammars

The Regulus grammar development toolset borrows ideas from several other systems, in particular the SRI Core Language Engine (CLE) and the Xerox Language Engine (XLE). The basic functionalities required are uncontroversial. As usual, the Regulus environment lets the user parse example sentences to create derivation trees and logical forms; in the other direction, if the grammar has also been compiled into a generator, the user can take a logical form and use it to generate a surface string and another derivation tree. Once a derivation tree has been created, either through parsing or through generation, it is possible to examine individual nodes to view the information associated with each one. Currently, this information consists of the syntactic features, the piece of logical form built up at the node, and the grammar rule or lexical entry used to create it.

The Regulus environment also provides a more elaborate debugging tool, which extends the earlier "grammar stepper" implemented under the CLE project. Typically, a grammar development problem has the following form. The user finds a bad sentence B which fails to get a correct parse; however, there are several apparently similar or related sentences $G_1...G_n$ which do get correct parses. In most cases, the explanation is that some rule which would appear in the intended parse for B has an incorrect feature-assignment.

A simple strategy for investigating problems of this kind is just to examine the structures of B and $G_1...G_n$ by eye, and attempt to determine what the crucial difference is. An experienced developer, who is closely familiar with the structure of the grammar, will quite often be able to solve the problem in this way, at least in simple cases. "Solving by inspection" is not, however, very systematic, and with complex rule bugs it can be hard even for experts to find the offending feature assignment. The larger the grammar becomes, especially in terms of the average number of features per category, the more challenging the *ad hoc* debugging approach becomes.

A more systematic strategy was pioneered in the CLE grammar stepper. The developer begins by looking at the working examples $G_1...G_n$, to determine what the intended correct structure would be for B. They then build up the corresponding structure for the bad example, starting at the bottom with the lexical items and manually selecting the rules used to combine them. At some point, a unification will fail, and this will normally reveal the bad feature assignment. The problem is that manual bottom-up construction of the derivation tree is very time-consuming, since even quite simple trees will usually have at least a dozen nodes.

The improved strategy used in the Regulus grammar stepper relies on the fact that the $G_1...G_n$ can usually be constructed to include all the individual pieces of the intended derivation tree for B, since in most cases the feature mis-match arises when combining two subtrees which are each internally consistent. We exploit this fact by allowing the developer to build up the tree for B by cutting up the trees for $G_1...G_n$ into smaller pieces, and then attempting to recombine them. Most often, it is enough to take two of the G_i, cut an appropriate subtree out of each one, and try to unify them together; this means that the developer can construct the tree for B with only five operations (two parses, two cuts, and a join), rather than requiring one operation for each node in B, as in the bottom-up approach.

A common pattern is that B and G_1 are identical, except for one noun-phrase constituent NP, and G_2 consists of NP on its own. To take an example from the MedSLT domain, B could be "does the morning

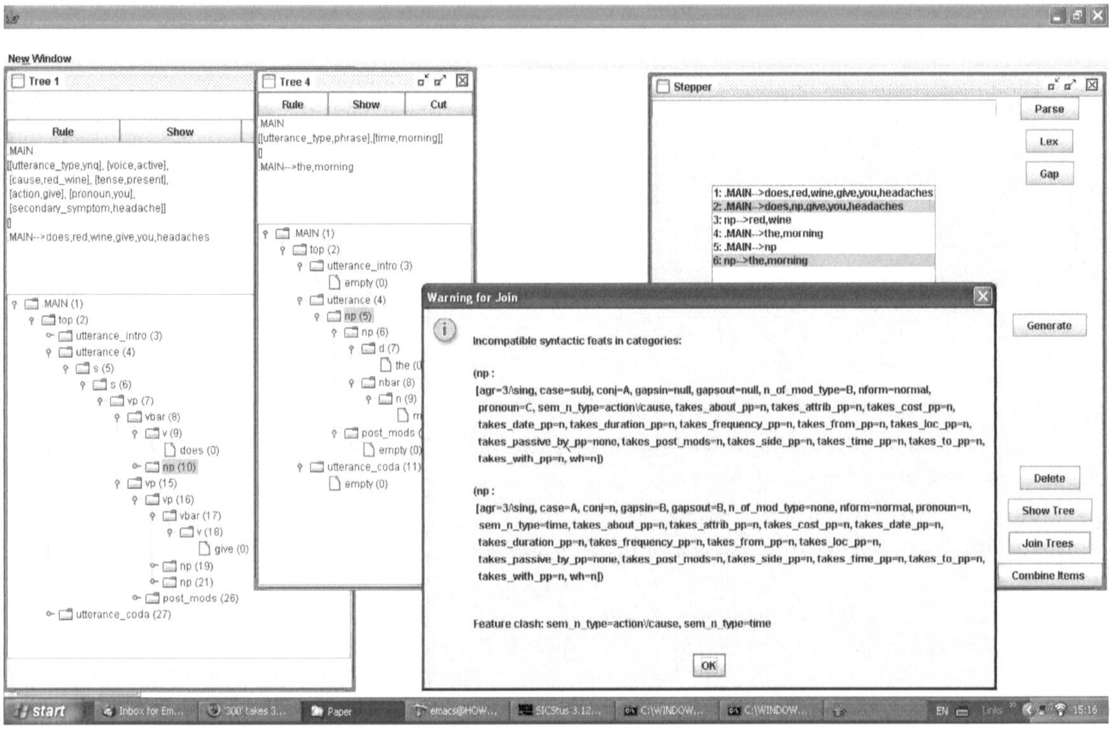

Figure 1: Example of using the grammar stepper to discover a feature mismatch. The window on the right headed "Stepper" presents the list of available trees, together with the controls. The windows headed "Tree 1" and "Tree 4" present the trees for item 1 ("does red wine give you headaches") and item 4 ("the morning"). The popup window on the lower right presents the feature mismatch information.

give you headaches?", G_1 the similar sentence "does red wine give you headaches?" and G_2 the single NP "the morning". We cut out the first NP subtree from G_1 to produce what is in effect a tree with an NP "slash category", that can be rendered as "does NP give you headaches?"; call this G'_1. We then cut out the single NP subtree (this accounts for most, but not all, of the derivation) from G_2, to produce G'_2. By attempting to unify G'_2 with the NP "hole" left in G'_1, we can determine the exact nature of the feature mismatch. We discover that the problem is in the sortal features: the value of the sortal feature on G'_2 is `time`, but the corresponding feature-value in the NP "hole" is `action\/cause`.

Figure 1 contains a screenshot of the development environment in the example above, showing the state when the feature mismatch is revealed. A detailed example, including screenshots for each step, is included in the online Regulus GUI tutorial[4].

3 Developing applications

The Regulus platform contains support for both speech translation and spoken dialogue applications. In each case, it is possible to run the development top-loop in a mode appropriate to the type of application, including carrying out systematic regression testing using both text and speech input. For both types of application, the platform assumes a uniform architecture with pre-specified levels of representation.

Due to shortage of space, and because it is the better-developed of the two, we focus on speech translation. The framework is interlingua-based, and also permits simple context-based translation involving resolution of ellipsis[5]. Processing goes through the following sequence of representations:

1. Spoken utterance in source language.

2. Recognised words in source language.

[4] Available in the file doc/RegulusGUITutorial.pdf from the SourceForge Regulus website

[5] Although it is often possible to translate ellipsis as ellipsis in closely related language pairs, this is usually not correct in more widely separated ones.

3. Source logical form. Source logical form and all other levels of representation are (almost) flat lists of attribute/value pairs.

4. "Source discourse representation". A regularised version of the source logical form, suitable for carrying out ellipsis resolution.

5. "Resolved source discourse representation". The output resulting from carrying out any necessary ellipsis processing on the source discourse representation. Typically this will add material from the preceding context representation to create a representation of a complete clause.

6. Interlingua. A language-independent version of the representation.

7. Target logical form.

8. Surface words in target language.

The transformations from source logical form to source discourse representation, from resolved source discourse representation to interlingua, and from interlinga to target logical form are defined using translation rules which map lists of attribute/value pairs to lists of attribute/value pairs. The translation trace includes all the levels of representation listed above, the translation rules used at each stage, and other information omitted here. The "translation mode" window provided by the development environment makes all these fields available in a structured form which allows the user to select for display only those that are currently of interest. The framework for spoken dialogue systems is similar, except that in the last three steps "Interlingua" is replaced by "Dialogue move", "Target logical form" by "Abstract response", and "Surface words in target language" by "Concrete response".

The platform contains tools for performing systematic regression testing of both speech translation and spoken dialogue applications, using both text and speech input. Input in the required modality is taken from a specified file and passed through all stages of processing, with the output being written to another file. The user is able to annotate the results with respect to correctness (the GUI presents a simple menu-based interface for doing this) and save the judgements permanently, so that they can be reused for future runs.

The most interesting aspects of the framework involve development of spoken dialogue systems. With many other spoken dialogue systems, the effect of a dialogue move is distributed throughout the program state, and true regression testing is very difficult. Here, our side-effect free approach to dialogue management means that the DM can be tested straightforwardly as an isolated component, since the context is fully encapsulated as an object. The theoretical issues involved are explored further in (Rayner and Hockey, 2004).

References

[Bouillon et al.2005] P. Bouillon, M. Rayner, N. Chatzichrisafis, B.A. Hockey, M. Santaholma, M. Starlander, Y. Nakao, K. Kanzaki, and H. Isahara. 2005. A generic multi-lingual open source platform for limited-domain medical speech translation. In *Proceedings of the 10th Conference of the European Association for Machine Translation (EAMT)*, pages 50–58, Budapest, Hungary.

[Rayner and Hockey2004] M. Rayner and B.A. Hockey. 2004. Side effect free dialogue management in a voice enabled procedure browser. In *Proceedings of the 8th International Conference on Spoken Language Processing (ICSLP)*, Jeju Island, Korea.

[Rayner et al.2005a] M. Rayner, P. Bouillon, N. Chatzichrisafis, B.A. Hockey, M. Santaholma, M. Starlander, H. Isahara, K. Kanzaki, and Y. Nakao. 2005a. Methodology for comparing grammar-based and robust approaches to speech understanding. In *Proceedings of the 9th International Conference on Spoken Language Processing (ICSLP)*, pages 1103–1107, Lisboa, Portugal.

[Rayner et al.2005b] M. Rayner, B.A. Hockey, J.M. Renders, N. Chatzichrisafis, and K. Farrell. 2005b. A voice enabled procedure browser for the international space station. In *Proceedings of the 43rd Annual Meeting of the Association for Computational Linguistics (interactive poster and demo track)*, Ann Arbor, MI.

[Rayner et al.2006] M. Rayner, B.A. Hockey, and P. Bouillon. 2006. *Putting Linguistics into Speech Recognition: The Regulus Grammar Compiler.* CSLI Press, Chicago.

Author Index